My Name is Brett
Truths from a
Trans Christian

by Brett Ray

Edited & Designed by:

Kathrin DePue, The Writing Mechanic

My Name is Brett: Truths from a Trans Christian

The Introduction

I suppose I always knew I would churn out a book someday. It has been my dream since I was a young child writing children's books in the backseat of my parents' car just to pass the time. But what I didn't expect was to write one this soon…or to write it about myself. The truth is, I'm not totally convinced that I'm the best person to tell this story, nor am I convinced that my story is the best one to tell.

But I also know I have no option but to let these words flow from me.

I have to share my life in these words because there are too many transgender men and women, boys and girls, and everyone in between and outside of that, who can't share their stories. There are too many transgender people who are unable to articulate their stories because they've been told their stories are wrong. There are too many transgender people who are unable to share their stories—even if they know they're true—because they fear for their lives. There are too many transgender people who are unable to tell their stories because they've already lost their lives due to transphobic violence or self-harm.

Tonight, I sit in the warm comfort of my North Carolina home; nine times out of ten, I don't have these fears. Most of the time, I feel safe. And so I have to write this story down because I *can*. That said, my voice is just a drop in the pond; it is not a reflection of every transgender person's experience. In fact, I am confident that I am among the more privileged in the transgender community, and, thus, my own narrative isn't all there is to the story. But I tell it in hopes that doing so creates a little more space for others to start telling their own stories. I tell it in hopes that people will read it and hear it and seek out the stories of other transgender people. I write it in hopes that the people who haven't might start searching to know their own stories.

I also write it selfishly. I write it because I have hopes that putting these words in ink will help me remember how to claim them as my own. Even as a trans man who is largely safe and supported, it's hard to know how to claim my story as my own when much of the world tells me my story isn't true. I write it for liberation from the words of doubt that others and I plant in my head.

In what follows, I may say things that make you uncomfortable. (Family members, if you're reading this, please know that you will undoubtedly be uncomfortable at times. I'm warning you now.) I ask that when that happens, you push yourself to figure out why.

Lastly, if you have questions or comments, please don't hesitate to write me. I will do my best to respond to each and every one of you.

Brett Ray
Durham, NC
June 2015

Acknowledgments

Though I penned the words in these pages, none of them would have been possible without the help of many lovely people, some of whom are listed here.

I want to thank Layne Martin for the years of love and support, but most importantly for the word "ambling"; lizzie mcmanus for the great wisdom, patience, and help with publicity; Jonathan David DePue for putting up with my constant fears and for being the best man I know (I love you, brother); Kathrin DePue for being the best editor around and for sharing her husband with me more than any woman should have to; Becky, Max, James, and Daniel Blalock for letting me claim them as my own and for claiming me right back; Nancy Kollhoff for the years of mentoring, love, and, most importantly, hope; Stephanie Neve for encouraging me and making sure I knew I was loved even in my darkest times; Mark Gammon and Eva Jablonski for putting up with my ridiculousness and for their humor, love, and ability to produce a beautiful baby girl; Trinity United Methodist Church/Las Americas Comunidad de Fe in Des Moines, IA for showing me that there is a place for me in the Church; Dr. Chuck Campbell for having all of the right words at all of the right times; Jan and JR for everything...there are no sufficient words for all you have done for me; my Papa and Grandma Vicki for showing me what it means to model your life after the love of Christ; and lastly, Mama and Larry for always welcoming me home with arms wide open...and with chicken strips on the table.

The Dedication

To my Aunt Ginger, the first person to say I finally looked like myself.

~

To my Mama, who never left my side; I love you.

~

To Jon, my brother, my best friend, and the man who repeatedly saves my life.

~

And to you, transgender reader, because you are courageous and worthy of love. Live boldly and love well.

Dear,

Before tonight, I'd never written a love letter.
Before tonight, I tried to ink my love to you, but a
lover does not love make, so instead I wrote fear.
I wrote the fear of being alone
and the fear of not being enough
and the fear of being way too much.
I wrote the fear that I had never existed without.

Until tonight.
Tonight, I write a love letter to the lover I never
expected
I would be able to rest my fingers on:
Myself.

Dear Self,
Your hands, they rest on your chest,
that part of you you'd go months without looking at,
and here, now, your hands find a home.

What used to be the cause of tear after tear,

those breasts,

now they are pecs,

and you can't stop looking at them with the eyes of a
lover.

I swear, if you could look in the eyes of the two
most in-love men,

they'd look like the eyes of murderers compared to
yours.

And honey, your voice is deep.

It's not the smooth, sexy baritone you always thought
it'd be,

but it's the perfect amount of deep for me.

When you sing, I can hear your heart in a way

it never spoke before, and every time your lips

have the courage to speak your truth,

I know you're speaking to me.

There are still lines on your chest from where they cut
you open,

or better yet, where they sewed you shut,

and there's a band-aid on your leg where you prick
yourself
with the needle that puts hair on your face.
And you, you're still a mountain range
with highs higher than the highest of heights
and lows that go so low you could swear they've never
seen the sunshine
but the difference — the difference now is that
you don't want or need a way out.

So tonight, I write a truth to you that sits deeper
in me than anything has before:

I love you.
Love,
Me.

Table of Contents

Chapter One

The Day

I never knew the power of writing or speaking until the day my words lost their ability to leave my throat. They just sat behind my tongue like a lake behind a dam—waves lapping against the wall, incapable of tearing it down. That day, I had more words floating in my head than I knew what to do with and they were driving me crazy. They eventually made their way out through my tear ducts.

It was September 9, 2011. I was a sophomore at a tiny liberal arts college in small-town Iowa, and I had just sat through the class that would change the rest of my life. I know people say that a lot—that classes or professors change their lives—but this class on this particular day really did turn my entire life on its head.

I didn't want to be there; in fact, I had thought about skipping out. It was a beautiful day and I'd have much rather been hitting the trails on my bicycle or heading down to the local ice cream parlor. But instead, I made my trek up the four flights of steep stairs to Wallace 401 — a classroom I will never forget, both for its involvement in this experience and because I always dreaded having to climb up there. There were probably fifteen people in this gender studies class, only two of whom identified as men at the time. It was discussion-based, so we largely read books and spent the entire two hours of every class time talking about them. This day, we had read a chapter of a book about the history of the treatment of women during their menstrual cycles.

Now, an important thing to realize at this point in my story is that everyone (myself sort of included) thought that I was a young woman. I presented as a female—albeit a tomboy—and I was using my original female name.

We were deep in this conversation about menstrual cycles and everyone else was talking, including the men, but I was silent. The women were mostly talking about their experiences in a way that claimed their menstrual cycles as their own; it was a part of their lives that they knew and lived and thought about. The men were mostly clueless—not in a bad way, just clueless in that they had never experienced a menstrual cycle. They had no idea what it would be like for their bodies to function that way, let alone how others would treat them if their bodies *did* function that way. The book and conversation were shocking for them.

What I realized during that discussion is that I had never felt more disconnected from myself in my life. I sat and listened to these women sharing their stories, and I had this overpowering sense that their stories were not my own. Yes, I had experienced a menstrual cycle before, but my experience was nothing like theirs. My experience was always one I tried to block out; it was dysphoric and hated. It was never something that just *was,* but it was always something that should *not* be.

It was then that my voice stopped working. It was then that I was afraid to make eye contact with anyone around the tables for fear that they would realize what I had just realized. It was then that I realized I was not a woman; I was, and always had been, male.

After class I nearly ran to my car and sobbed because the dark ball in my gut that had been welling up inside of me for my entire life had finally come into light. I knew that, even if I wanted to, I couldn't put it back in the shadows again.

The Aftermath

Realizing the truth about yourself can be one of the most terrifying and lonely events you ever experience. Especially when said truth comes with more questions than answers. And as I sat in my car that fall day after class, I faced the most difficult question of my life. It was no longer, "Could this be true?" It was, "This is true. I am a transgender man. Am I going to live with that fact, or am I going to stop my life right here?"

I wondered if I would hammer the last nail in my own coffin. Would the truth about my life be scary enough to end it?

It wasn't the first time I had asked myself that question. I had struggled with depression and anxiety for much of my life, and it came to a head that previous summer. During that summer, my days usually consisted of going to work and spending most of my free time watching the Disney Channel while searching Google for the most convenient, efficient, and painless way to die. The irony of that is not lost on me. One night I ingested as many pills as I could manage to force down my throat in hopes that the cycle I was in could stop. Instead, I woke up the next morning in my bed with a horrible, horrible stomachache. Thank God for that.

And thank God for cell phones. Because as I sat in my car, head on my steering wheel, bawling, and wondering what would become of my life, I felt my phone vibrate in my pocket. Amid the tears, I pulled it out. I can't tell you who texted me or what they said, but seeing that device in my hand made me remember how to make a phone call.

I called one of my professors, mentors, and chosen-family-members, and like always, she answered. I asked if I could go out to her farm because there was something I needed to talk about. And, like always, she said yes.

This professor had been there for me in incredible ways since my first day of college—actually, since even before then. When I visited campus as an anticipated religion major, she was the one who had to field all of my father's questions about the job market and income potential. Clearly she did a good job, as I ended up in the religion department at her school.

But more than that, my first year, as it is for many students, was a time of self-exploration and revelation. Some of the exploration I put myself through was painful and unhealthy. This professor and her spouse were there for that because they understood it in a way most people didn't. And some of the exploration I put myself through was painful, but necessary and ultimately liberating. They were there for that, too, because as queer people, they understood it in a way many people didn't. The exploration that falls in the latter camp—that is, painful but necessary—was mostly my exploration of my sexual orientation.

If I recall correctly, I think it only took me one weekend away at college to have my first drunken make-out session with a girl. (Sorry, Mom.) I didn't think that made me a lesbian (keep in mind that I and everyone else thought I was a woman at the time), but I knew it changed things for me.

As my first semester went on, I fell in love with my at-the-time best friend. This wasn't young, puppy love either. This was the real deal that I am confident some people don't experience in their entire lives. Let's call this friend and lover Grace because she always showed me much more grace than was ever warranted. As it turned out, she was in love with me, too. Being in love with a woman was scary for the both of us, but my professor and her partner helped us navigate those feelings of transitioning from best friends to partners. They helped us when we were living in the closet, they helped us come out of the closet, and they showed us how to love each other publicly. They taught us how to argue in a healthy way and how to think about what we could give to the world as a couple that neither of us could give on our own. They helped us celebrate our engagement. They helped us tell our uncertain families about our engagement. And, eventually, they helped support each of us when that engagement fell to pieces, which happened the same summer I tried to swallow my life away in a bottle of pills.

I knew that if there was one place I could go to process all of this—being a trans man and not knowing whether that would mean living or dying—it would be their farm. So I drove myself out there; I'll never forget the way my shaking hands and legs calmed down when I saw them waiting for me in their front yard. My professor was up on the ladder working on the gutters and her partner was waving at me. As I pulled into their driveway, I felt like I was catching myself from a potential fall—feeling the full force of the adrenaline rush, but knowing I was safe.

Neither of them are much for bullshit small-talk, which is perfect for me because I hate small-talk. However, I could live in it if it meant not having to deal with the hard stuff. I got out of my car, walked over to them, hugged each one of them, and as I embraced them, they said, "So, what's going on?" That wasn't the "what's up" kind of "what's going on"; it was the "something serious is obviously going on, so let's talk about it—now" kind. I explained my class experience as best as I could, and at the end of my story I said, "Am I crazy?"

They looked at me, and then looked each other in the eyes as if to ask who should take the lead on this one. I think it was my professor's spouse who looked back to me first and said, "Absolutely not.

It makes sense. We have actually talked about how we wondered if this would be a part of your story." Hearing those words allowed me to truly exhale for the first time since I had realized I was transgender.

I spent the next hour word-vomiting all of my fears on them. They listened patiently. I can't remember all of their words or their looks or their hugs. But I remember the way it felt to have a safe space to lay everything on the table. I remember the way it felt for me to name my fears: Would my family love me? Would my church accept me? Was God okay with this? Would I ever find a job? Would my friends stick with me? Would I ever be able to find someone to love me again? They didn't tell me my fears were wrong; they encouraged me and let me claim my fears as real, present feelings.

But they also showed me their excitement. They reminded me how exciting it is to be in the place of knowing oneself, even if it is scary. They reminded me that it's exciting to be in tune with oneself. They reminded me that they will always walk alongside me.

And then they asked, "What should we call you?"

The Name

"My name is Brett, and I'm an alcoholic."

I've introduced myself that way in many dingy church basements, fellowship halls, Wesley buildings, and Alano clubs. I've done so in the states of Iowa, Colorado, Virginia, Kansas, and North Carolina at least. In Alcoholics Anonymous, no matter where you go, you can always expect the same thing—a group of misfits trying to stay sober. I've been one of those misfits for four years now.

One of my favorite parts about AA is the way we do introductions. I've found great joy in being welcomed into a group of people by name. In fact, I think AA is probably where I first learned how important names are. But of course, my AA family didn't always greet me as Brett. For six months, their response to my introduction was always, "Hi, Bri."

I remember clearly the day they all looked at me and called me Brett for the first time. It was terrifying and amazing all at the same time.

The meeting was a "discussion" meeting, which meant that the chair-person read a short devotion and then shared a few thoughts about the reading. After that, we would go around the circle while each of us shared a thought about the devotion or about anything pertaining to our sobriety. I remember that night being a particularly full meeting with maybe twenty-to-thirty people in attendance. (For us, that was a full meeting.) Almost all of the "regulars" were there, and a handful of "newbies" and visitors filled the gaps. I was so glad it was full; maybe I could make my announcement to this group at one time without suffering through the awkwardness of giving it out to handfuls of people a ton of different times. I didn't know back then the extent to which this conversation would reappear in my life. And little did I know that someday I would actually enjoy telling it.

That night, my story did not come with joy and excitement; it came with trembling legs, a lump in my throat, and sweaty palms. I was so afraid to admit—even to the people who already knew the best and worst about me—that I truly was (am) Brett. It's not that I worried much about what they thought of me. I didn't. What I worried about was what it would mean for them to take me seriously. I worried about the power my words would have over me once I gave them enough validity to speak them to my main community of support.

In the program, we have this concept of "leaving things in the room." Basically, it's the idea that if you come to a meeting and talk about situations that consume your mind and threaten your sobriety, then they will begin to lose their power over you. I don't know how it works, but time and time again, I've experienced the way that vocalizing these issues makes them loosen their grip on me. Along with this, I know that the words we use to speak about ourselves matter. I know that when I tell myself I'm not good enough for something, it sinks deep inside me and breaks a place that is so hard to repair. I know that when I started telling myself I was smart, I saw radical changes in my abilities, and I started to care less about whether or not other people thought I was smart.

But I didn't know what sharing these words would do to me. If they took me seriously, would it affirm my identity to myself? Or, would it make my true self so real to me that I wouldn't know how to handle it? These were questions to which I had no answer, but I knew I needed to tell the group who I was anyway.

The meeting was held in the basement of a Wesley house at a local university. We were all gathered on couches and recliners, and most of us drank coffee and ate cookies. I normally partook in the pre-meeting banter and the coffee drinking. That night, I was silent and I didn't dare put any caffeine into my body for fear of feeding my anxiety further until it spun out of control. I can't tell you a single thing that was said in that meeting before it was my turn to talk; I spent the entire time rehearsing my speech over and over in my head. If I was only doing this once, it had to be perfect.

Most AA meetings only last an hour, and we were about 45 minutes into the meeting before it was finally my turn to share. My throat was dry and my hands were soaked with sweat. They were fidgeting uncontrollably. I couldn't manage to look anyone in the eyes, so I alternated making eye contact with the ceiling and then the floor as I introduced myself: "My name is Bri, and I'm an alcoholic."

"Hi, Bri."

With a shaky voice I said something like this:

"I don't really have much to say about the topic, but there is something important that I need to let you all in on. I know I've only been in the program a few months at this point, but I've already learned so much about myself. It's amazing what a few days without vodka can do." We all chuckled a little at that. It's funny because it sounds ridiculous, but it's so true for us.

"Anyway, I've recently come to a fairly significant realization about myself. I think, um, you know, part of why I used to drink was because I was afraid of who I was. I was afraid that if I was my true self, people wouldn't love me. But what I've learned here is that there *are* people who will love me as myself. And besides that, I don't have control over who likes me and who doesn't like me; I just know I have to be myself. So I have to be honest with you. I've been living as 'Bri' for my entire life, but it's never felt right. I've never been good at being a girl and I've never been good at being 'Bri.' So from here on out, I'm not going to do that anymore; it's not me. From here on out, I'm going to go by the name Brett and live as Brett. Today I'm grateful to be sober because I'm not quite as afraid to confront myself anymore. It's still scary, but, y'know, it's possible now. I'm grateful for you all. Thanks for accepting me as I am. And with that, I'll pass."

"Thanks, Brett. We're glad you're here."

They responded without missing a beat. I was prepared for a jumbled mess of some people calling me Brett and some people calling me Bri. I was ready for people to just be confused and not respond at all. I realized when I was finished that I never actually told them I was transgender. I didn't go into much detail at all. I just told them that I was Brett, and they listened to me, respected me for it, and granted my wish to be called Brett.

"Thanks, Brett. We're glad you're here."

I can't tell you how formational those words were for me. Coming out to people, even people I trust and love, is one of the hardest things I'll ever do. And honestly, so far anyway, it's never really gotten easier. The nerves are always there, even if I'm confident I will be received well. I'm basically putting myself in someone else's hands, knowing that they can do with me whatever they wish— knowing that when I tell them who I am, they are faced with two options: loving me or rejecting me. And they will choose one option or the other. There are no in-betweens. When I come out, I'm trusting people to make their own decision about whether or not they want to walk this road with me; I'm trusting them to decide whether or not I am worth the potholes, tears, awkward silences, unknowns, and detours that are bound to come up on this journey. In coming out, I'm trusting them and I'm asking them to trust and love me, too.

This kind of response of gratitude that my AA community gave me was the best I could have hoped for. No, it was better than the best I could have hoped for. I placed the truth about myself in their hands and they said, "Thanks, Brett. We're glad you're here."

During a time in my life when I was not always so glad to be there—in the rooms of AA or in the body of a trans man—hearing others tell me *they* were glad I was there was crucial. So now, whenever people come out to me, I try to tell them thank you. I try to tell them thanks for trusting me with their true selves—thanks for living into the truth about themselves. Most importantly, though, I tell them that I am glad they are here as they are. Those words are often far more vital than we realize.

When I came out to my AA community, I was not as aware of the kind of significance of all of the words shared in that meeting as I am now. At the time, I didn't know what I was leaving in the room and what I was taking with me. I wasn't sure *who* I was leaving in the room and who I was taking with me.

But today, I see that by speaking my truth in that room, I was laying down all of my paralyzing fear that was keeping me from moving forward. I was laying down the dark parts of my head that I used to drink away instead of explore. I was laying down my lies about myself that I had been telling for so long. I was laying down the belief that being Brett wasn't good enough. I was laying down my desire to hide. I was laying down the parts of my old self that had a death grip on me and I was leaving her in the room.

All the while, I was picking up the courage and love for which I had been yearning for so long. I was picking up the confidence to be myself. I was picking up the ability to trust myself. I was picking up the love of my friends. And, most importantly, I was picking up the building blocks for the self-love that I would soon start constructing.

To this day, I carry those words with me. And on the days when I forget what it means to love myself, I remember them, and I, too, thank myself for being here.

The Cousins

For many trans people, names are a very personal matter (and rightfully so). You see, being called the wrong thing for huge portions of your life is painful. Most of the time, when people call someone by their birth name, they're not trying to be mean; that's just how we talk to people. But for trans people who don't yet have the language or safe space to acknowledge why their birth names are so wrong, the pain just sits inside, building up and up. So when we finally get to a place where we can acknowledge the way in which we *actually* want to be addressed, hearing our old name or having people question us about our new name can feel invasive and hurtful.

I say all of this in preface to the story of why I chose the name Brett for myself. Throughout my transition, I have chosen to be very transparent about who I am and why I have done the things I have done. Because of this, many people have asked me about my names—both my old name and why I chose my new name. For me, this is fine; I'm comfortable with those questions. But I think it's important to acknowledge that for trans people, there is a lot of vulnerability wrapped up in our names. It's important that others respect that vulnerability and tenderness. More specifically, it's not always appropriate to ask trans people about what their old name was or why they have this new name now. Please, for the sake of your trans friends, tread lightly with questions; ask yourself if the potential harm your questioning may cause is worth appeasing your sense of curiosity.

All that said, I enjoy it when people ask me questions, particularly about the story of how and why I chose my name. In fact, at the risk of sounding arrogant, I'm quite fond of my name and the way I chose it; I think it's clever and true to myself. (Which is the point, after all, right?)

Growing up, mine was a split family. I lived as an only child with my mama and my step-dad, but I had a half-sister who lived with my biological dad. (I now have a handful of lovely stepsiblings, too.) For a while, I visited my dad and sister on a somewhat regular basis, but as the years went on, and I went to school and started playing sports (all of the sports), the visits were reduced to birthday and Christmas e-mails.

For most of my life, then, I lived as an only child. I've heard many complaints to and from only children. According to people who aren't only children, we are selfish and always grow up with problems. While I don't think that actually has anything to do with being an only child, I'm not really the shining example to refute that claim.

Often, according to only children, the only-child life is depicted as boring and lonely. Despite the fact that I used to beg my parents for a baby brother, I quite enjoyed the only-child life as it meant I didn't have to worry about my siblings' schedules. My sports and school events were the only ones we worried about, and I loved that. Like I said, I'm no shining example of a selfless only child. (Side note: Somewhere along the line, I learned that if you stand in a fairy ring and make a wish, it would come true. And, as it happened, we had a fairy ring near our backyard. So as a five- or six-year-old, my parents would regularly find me standing in the fairy ring, wishing for a baby brother. I was an odd but lovable child.)

Maybe if I had been all alone, I wouldn't have enjoyed being an only-child as much, but I had three cousins who lived no more than an hour and a half away for my entire childhood. I am the oldest, Rachelle is two years younger than me, Kelsey almost two years younger than her, and Lance almost two years younger than Kelsey. We were always pretty close; since I didn't really know what it was like to have siblings, they were the closest I had.

Whenever we had family gatherings, we did what most kids do: avoid the adults. We would immediately sprint to the basement or toy room of whatever house we were in to get lost in our own fantasy worlds in which we were the adults—the people in charge. Usually, it would be some combination of playing house or cops and robbers. (I always had a fascination with being a police officer.)

Though the situations in our games changed often, our characters almost always remained the same. Lance was always the baby. He was never super excited about being the baby because that was his real life, too, but he was too small to have a say. He would either be who and what we wanted him to be or he wasn't going to play with us. For some reason, he always wanted to play with us. So he was the baby and we would dress him up and boss him around and push him through the house in our dolls' strollers.

Kelsey was the middle sibling in our make-believe world and Rachelle was usually the mom. I'm realizing as I write this that almost none of us were playing roles that were entirely different from our reality...except for me. I always played the badass oldest brother. Sometimes I pretended to be a weight-lifter who juggled multiple girlfriends. I sometimes played a really smart college student who wanted to be a professor, other times I was a writer, and sometimes I was a drug addict who was stuck at home because I had no money. What remained consistent, though, was that my name was always Brett.

My cousins and I had worked out a deal back then that I don't even know if they remember: whenever we'd play these games, they weren't allowed to tell any grown-ups about my character. And, really, when I was ten years old playing the role of a drug addict, that was probably a great decision. I imagine I might have lost some TV privileges if my parents had known what was going on.

Inhabiting this make-believe world was a way for me to be the person I wanted to be. But to me, the game was always real. In some ways, being Brett in those "make-believe" situations felt more *real* than my real life. And because of that, because of how real I knew it was, I was fearful of how easy it could be for my family to see how badly I wanted our games of house to be my actual life. But I was nowhere near ready for my family to know that, and so my cousins weren't allowed to tell anyone. I didn't want anyone to know that my imagination was capable of thinking of myself as a boy.

Even though I always felt on-edge about being "found out," I don't think any of my other family members had a clue at the time. I doubt my family would have "figured me out" even if my cousins had told everyone that I was always a boy when we played.

But even at such a young age, I had the instinct to be fearful. I was afraid of what my family would do if they found out, and I was afraid of being seen as different. I knew I was Brett, even back then, but I didn't *know* it enough to feel comfortable with everyone else knowing it, too. I didn't *know* it enough to have the language to talk about it. And so Brett just lived in parsonage basements and out in the country when we would run around without the adults. Brett lived in my head and my dreams as the man I would someday grow into. But Brett lived. Even back then, Brett lived.

Once I had the words to tell others (and myself) that I was a trans man, I knew Brett would be my name. Brett has always been my name. Today, whenever someone calls me Brett or when I put my name on anything, I'm drawn back into the life of a little boy who was just wishing things would get better. I flash back to the life of a little boy who wished he could live his life outside of the confines of secret games and hiding places—a little boy who just wanted to live as himself. My name is Brett because I want to remember that I've always been that little boy; he still lives in me. I'm Brett so that I remember that I was right, even back then, to know that Brett—that I—am very much real, very much alive, and that my story is very much true.

Chapter Two

The Home

When I left for college, I went looking for a new beginning to a new life. I had no idea just what kind of new beginning I was in for, but I was certain there would be one. High school was not ideal for me. (But, really, is it ideal for anyone?) I had many friends, my grades were fine, most of my teachers loved me, and I had fun on the swim team. The cool kids invited me to their parties, and I wasn't even too awkward when I showed up. My friends and I spent time on the beach at the lake. We pondered life's great questions—whether God was near or far—drank beer, skipped rocks, and caught fish. My parents didn't have too many rules for me, but I'm sure if they knew all that I was up to back then, they probably would have made more. The point is, on paper, my four years of high school were probably better than most.

But high school was not good for me — or I for it. Depression and anxiety ran rampant in me. I didn't know how to talk about them or how to ask for help. I only knew that I would frequently get sick because of how anxious I was. I would plan the timing of my meals around when I thought I would have the time and space to get sick if need be. It was no way to live.

My high school years were also filled with drinking and smoking and all of the things parents wish their kids would stay away from. I never got arrested, and I didn't think I was getting hurt or hurting anyone else. But I also knew that no matter how much I drank, how many parties I went to, no matter how many lies I told, or people I hooked up with, I wasn't happy. And in that Kansas town, I never would be.

So when it was time to apply for colleges, my sights were set on any school that wasn't in Kansas. My dad worked at the university in my hometown, and because of that, I could have gone to school without taking out loans. But I would have no part of that. (Now that I have loans from a private undergrad and a private graduate school, my wallet kicks me for that decision, but I don't actually regret it one bit.) Going to the university in that town would have been just like going to high school for another four years, and I barely made it out of the first four without major incident. Four more could have—likely would have—destroyed me.

The school I ended up going to was about five hours from home—just close enough that if I needed to go back for a weekend I could but far enough that I was keenly aware of my independence. I didn't know a single person who would be there. Everyone who found that out felt sorry for me; I think they thought I was going to be lonely or something. But not knowing anyone—or, more precisely, having no one know me—was exactly what I wanted. I could be whoever I wanted to be. I didn't have to be the kid whose shoulder injury prevented her from doing the thing she loved most: swimming long-distance butterfly competitively. I didn't have to be the wild kid who drank too much (though, this habit certainly died hard). I didn't have to be the one liberal person among a group of conservative Christians. Maybe, instead, my liberal leanings would fit in, or I'd find a significant other, or I'd actually start to like school. Maybe I'd get even better grades and everyone would think I was smart. Or maybe I'd be known for my ability to write a mean slam poem. Maybe I'd start to sing for people.

I had all of these dreams about a new life I'd find at college, but I wasn't sure what it would look like. I knew I'd find friends, but I wasn't sure who they would be or what clique they'd put me in.

What I did know, though, was that unlike the hopes of many of my friends from home, I vowed to stay away from sororities. I was a tomboy; I didn't fit into all that girly, dressy-uppy, ditzy girl bullshit.

But then, in the first couple weeks of school, I made some good friends. Some great friends, actually. They were wonderful, lovely, hilarious, and oh so good to me. They invited me to their events, and they made sure I didn't have to do anything alone. They shared their secrets about how to navigate the first few weeks of school, and they gave the best hugs. And even though I wasn't at all homesick, I missed getting good hugs, damnit.

As it turns out, the three lovely women who claimed me for their friend group were all in the same sorority. A few weeks into the year, they told me they wanted me to join them, so I begrudgingly went to one of their informal recruiting nights. Surprisingly enough, I actually had fun. They all joked around with me and even genuinely laughed at some of my ridiculous jokes. Most importantly, though, they were fine with me hating the stupid crafts we were supposed to do.

They offered me a bid to join their sorority later that night. While I had always been adamant in my hatred for the Greek system, their offer was compelling; it would give me an identity in a place where I had yet to claim one. Plus, these women were wonderful, and they seemed to accept me in my goofy, cynical, and wild ways. How could I turn down an offer of acceptance and social status? I joined them.

That year, I continued living in the freshman dorms and really only went over to the house for the weekly meetings and occasional required social gatherings. I spent significant time with the ladies who recruited me, though. We were great friends, and I'm still friends with some of them.

They were even good to me when they learned that I was attracted to women and loved Grace. I was afraid of how they would handle that, as the Greek system is notoriously conservative, but these women were so good to me.

My sophomore year, though, I was required to live in the sorority house. It was just a part of being a member, but a sorority house is no place for a guy to live...

I don't really remember exactly how I told all of them that I was Brett. I think it happened over time; first I told the women who recruited me because I knew they would love me just the same. They were some of my most trusted people in my life. Then I told some people on the margins of my friend group and just relied on the gossip grapevines to do their job. And they did. I don't think word really traveled too far outside of the house, though, probably because there were enough people to talk to inside of the house and because they didn't want to admit to others that there was a trans man in their midst. They had a reputation to keep, after all.

I had a lot of conversations behind closed doors with three or four people at a time. I fielded all of their questions because I didn't know how to keep a space for myself there unless I was completely transparent and straightforward with them. To be honest, I think those early conversations were also me trying to make sense of everything for myself.

I remember the feeling I had when I realized that I was a guy living in an all-female house and how out of place I felt. It felt like I was constantly being misidentified—and constantly misidentifying myself. To live in a sorority, by definition, labeled me as a woman. How could I get myself, not to mention others, to really, fully believe that I was a man when I lived in a house that required all of its residents to be women? How could I be a man when the rules of the house required me to wear skirts to particular meetings? How could I be a man when people were still calling me Bri? Every time I heard people whispering about me, every time people asked insensitive questions, or the time I found out that my entire bed had been drenched in pitchers of beer, I wondered how I could ever be Brett. I sometimes just wanted to go back to being Bri, but I knew that wouldn't solve the problem.

But for some people in the house, telling them that my name was Brett was good enough for them; they immediately made the transition to calling to me Brett and were even better at being consistent with it than I was. I can think of multiple times when I'd accidentally start writing Bri on something and one of them would tap my shoulder and say, "Brett, your name is Brett." Or when I made a mistake on something and mumbled, "Damnit, Bri," a friend coughed and said, "You mean, 'Damnit, Brett.'"

I am infinitely grateful for my own mistakes and my friends' corrections. My own mistakes helped me remain realistic about my new name. Ideally, I know that if I ask someone to call me Brett, they should just be able to do it. But realistically, if I couldn't even get my own name right all of the time at the beginning of my transition, I knew that I couldn't expect everyone else to get it right all of the time. That doesn't mean that their errors weren't annoying and painful, but my own mistakes helped me understand them better. My friends' corrections showed me how hard they were trying to honor the person they knew I was. Most importantly, it showed me that they believed me. They believed I was Brett, and that it was good and right to call me Brett—even when I forgot myself.

That's what good friends do. They remind us who we are when we forget. And we do forget; we forget more often than we know or would like to admit. Sometimes we forget what we ought to call ourselves—loved, cared for, and cherished. We forget the stories that make us who we are and we think that somehow we got to our place in life on our own. We think that we are fuck-ups who will never be good enough. But our friends act as our mirrors and they tell us we are wrong. They remind us that we didn't get here alone, that we are good enough, that we are loved, and, sometimes, they softly speak our very names to us when we forget them. My friends' corrective acts spoke life into my name in a way that I didn't know was necessary, but that was absolutely vital.

I think there are two parts to being named: there's the act of naming—receiving your name from someone else or naming yourself—and then there's the act of that name gaining life through use. Before I used it for myself, "Brett" was just a word; it was just a word before my friends looked me in the eyes and said, "You are Brett now, and we know that." My name was given life when we started using it. Every time I was corrected, or every time someone called me Brett, I became a little bit more alive as "Brett."

It's not that their language changed who I was; it didn't. I am not more Brett—not more of a man—when people call me Brett, and I am no less a man when people refuse to acknowledge me as such. But their words do matter. My friends' affirmations, their telling of my own story back to me when I forgot, helped me to step more fully and completely into living as myself. Their corrections helped me take strides out of the lies that I had told myself for years—the lies that said I was a girl and the lies that said I was Bri. They no longer had interest in playing that game, and they knew that it was important I didn't play it anymore either.

For their courage in reminding me who I was back then and who I am now, I am eternally grateful.

The Facebook

Shortly after news of my name change had swept through the sorority, I felt like it was time to open up the floodgates and tell the rest of the people at school. But how does one do that? How does one clue hundreds of friends, professors, and acquaintances in on a name change? It's not something most people have experience with.

Unbeknownst to me at first, I was not the only trans man on campus. There was a man a year older than me who had transitioned before college. Luckily, my professor knew of him, and she put us in contact. Even luckier for me, he was more than willing to talk to me about what it's like to be trans and how he took those first steps.

I remember a few fall days when we walked around the town square and shared stories about our lives. We hardly knew each other, but the parallels in our stories were amazing. I had never quite connected like that to another person because no one else understood the trans part of me the way he did.

We talked about many aspects of transition: living situations at school, hormones, surgeries, families, friends, etc. But perhaps most helpful of our conversations was the advice he gave me about names.

I asked him how he went about telling everyone to call him by his name. I told him I didn't particularly want to have a conversation with everyone individually to get the word out; that wasn't feasible anyway. He was completely sympathetic to my worries and said he had felt the same way when he made his name change. So how did he do it? How does anyone in our generation do anything? Social media. He changed his name on Facebook and (if I remember correctly) made a brief status about how he would prefer people call him by that new name.

I was hesitant to follow suit because Facebook felt impersonal. Plus, my Facebook presence reached well beyond my community in Iowa and I wasn't sure I was ready for that. Yet, I was more willing to risk fielding questions from too many people than wait any longer to have those around me know who I was.

When I changed my name to Brett on Facebook and posted a brief status about why (which I also hid from anyone back home—thank God for privacy settings), most of the people in the sorority house liked it. In fact, a lot of people liked it. A like on Facebook is not an equivalent to understanding or being supportive, but seeing that response helped ease my worries—even if only briefly.

It didn't take long for the private messages to flood in. Some of them asked if they had missed something, some asked detailed questions, others offered words of support, and still others told me I was confused and that this wasn't what God wanted for my life. I tried to take them all in stride, but many of them simply fed my growing anxiety.

The community at my college was pretty liberal, and so I didn't have much trouble finding support. There were some fellow students who I knew talked about me behind my back, but they weren't people I was interested in being friends with anyway. My professors were great; they were always sure to call me by the right name. Every once in a while, they'd mess up my preferred pronouns. But they were always apologetic, and I knew them well enough to know that any time they messed up, it was legitimately an accident, not a passive-aggressive attempt at telling me I shouldn't be Brett.

I had most people in Iowa calling me Brett and knowing I was trans sooner than I expected. The quick turnaround between me knowing I was trans, knowing I wanted to be called Brett, and having that be a reality was amazing. Once I had figured out those pieces, every day that I *wasn't* being addressed as Brett with male pronouns got harder and harder. Seeing people jump on board so quickly was exactly what I needed.

But I was still living two lives.

Sure, the people at my school knew I was Brett. But my family and my friends back home had no idea, and I didn't know how to tell them. For months, I was Brett at school and Briana at home. Having a split-life was horrific. Most of the time I tried to pretend that my life at home wasn't real, but that just led to a familial disconnect that none of us wanted. And when my family did talk to me, I got angry. I was angry that they would call me Briana and "she." Couldn't they see that I wasn't that person? They couldn't, and I couldn't tell them. The anger was unwarranted, but it was real nonetheless.

In some ways, then, I had been liberated from the lie I was living because I had people calling me Brett; but, at the same time, I kept living two lives. There was the life I wanted, the life that I knew was true and real—the life in Iowa—and then there was the life that people at home still believed. From September 2011 until December 2011, I kept up my two lives—all the while keeping my family at a distance.

It was a long three months, and I regret keeping myself from my family as long as I did—and for blatantly lying to them on occasion—but the time helped me sort out some of the truths about myself. It helped me to figure out how to articulate who I was and what I was feeling. And if I was going to make it through what was to come next, that time of introspection was more than necessary.

The Letter

I knew I had to tell my family that I was Brett at some point, and I knew that it needed to be sooner rather than later. Living as two people is no way for a person to live. In many ways, a double life is easier than just being honest with everyone because honesty almost always comes with a price. But so does leading a double life, and, at some point, the cost of a double life becomes so high that it is no longer worth it. I remember always feeling on edge when my family didn't know that I was transitioning to Brett. Whenever I was open and honest with my community in Iowa, I feared that my truth would somehow make it back to my hometown and to my parents. And whenever I was at home or talking to my family, I felt on edge because I was afraid I'd let it slip. Even more than that, though, was the frustration—both on my side and the side of my family—about the fact that I no longer knew how to be the child and grandchild my family thought I was.

In some ways, I wasn't so different from the young person my family last saw. I still loved sports, playing my guitar, and talking and writing theology. I still loved people. I was still passionate about economic injustice and food insecurity. I still had friends. I still loved women (to the chagrin of some of my family). I had my same sense of humor. I still loved them. I was still that person.

But I was also nothing like the person they knew. My hair was shorter and my clothes were baggier. I was infinitely more aware of myself and my place in the world. I was more and more aware of gendered expectations in our family and, well, in everyone, and I was much more willing to transgress them. Those transgressions weren't always welcome. The more I knew myself, the more outspoken I became. Even though I wasn't a wholly new person, my family could sense that something was different—something that they couldn't tap into just yet.

At some point, the divide between Briana in Kansas and Brett in Iowa became too much for me to handle. I don't know when I made the decision that I needed to tell my parents, but it was sometime before Christmas break of 2011. Though many of my friends and loved ones in Iowa told me not to come out and therefore ruin Christmas break for the second year in a row, I decided Christmas break would be the best time to do it. (I've never been great at listening to others' advice. It's something I'm working on.)

I decided I would write my parents a letter explaining what was going on, give it to them, go out for about an hour, and then come back and talk to them. For some people, an actual conversation right away might be best, but I convey information best through writing. Speaking clearly is significantly harder for me, and I was also convinced that it'd be best if I wasn't there for my parents' initial reactions. I wanted them to have the space to react how they needed to react, and I knew that it might be good for all of us if I didn't see it.

I think I handed them the letter on a Sunday afternoon. We had just finished cleaning up from lunch and they were sitting on the couch relaxing and watching a cooking show. I passed the letter to my Mama and I said, "I have something I need you to read. And I'm going to go out shopping for a while, but then I'll be back so we can talk about it."

As soon as I got the words out of my mouth, I started bawling. I collapsed into my Mama—something I hadn't done in so long. She hugged me and she kissed my head and she said, "I don't know what's in this letter, but honey, I know that it's okay, and I know that I'm going to love you the same."

I appreciated her sentiment, but half of me didn't believe her. I told her I loved her too, got up, and left the house. I drove and cried for at least an hour and a half. I couldn't bring myself to go home. As I drove, my life was changing forever, and I knew it, but I didn't know exactly *how* it was going to change. My family could accept me, or they could kick me out. While most of me knew it would at least not be the latter, I wasn't wholly convinced. That kind of not knowing was one of the hardest parts of my entire transitional experience. I had half a mind to drive back to Iowa, but I knew that wasn't really fair to my parents. By that point, I had committed to having the conversation with them, no matter how painful or awkward it would be. I had no other option but to go through with it.

When I pulled into my driveway that Sunday afternoon, I was convinced I would never be able to leave my car. My body felt like it weighed a million pounds and my face was stiff with that I've-been-crying-for-hours feeling. I tried to take deep breaths and push down the puffiness surrounding my eyes. Finally, I peeled myself out of my car and trudged into the house.

My Mama heard me pull up and greeted me by the door with a huge hug and the words, "I love you so much."

Growing up, I didn't give my Mama enough credit for how great she was and is. Seriously, she's the best Mom I could have ever hoped for. In that hug, during which I was crying and she was simply showering me with love, I realized just how great she had always been to me.

Mama and I had a really good conversation after that. My dad had gone to work, and it would be years before we would ever talk about me being trans again. But I was thankful for the conversation I was able to have with my Mama.

She was so honest with me, which I needed and appreciated. She admitted that she understood where I was coming from, but, at the same time, she didn't understand at all.

Being trans wasn't ever something she had experienced, so it was hard for her to get it— especially since I was her child. I'm sympathetic to her inability to initially understand because she knew me before I knew myself. She held me in her arms as her baby girl, and she spent her entire adult life protecting me and trying to make sure I was healthy, happy, and safe. To find out that I wasn't always happy or healthy—and that, realistically, because I'm trans, I won't always be safe—had to be hard on her. I'm glad she knew that she could be honest with me about her fears for my life. I'm most appreciative, though, of how often she told me she loved me.

As a part of that conversation, she told me that she was not ready to call me Brett or use male pronouns yet. That was a difficult thing to hear, but I expected it. And the fact that she even included "yet" in her statement was enough for me. That gave me the hope that someday it wouldn't be this way. I assured her I knew it was a process and that I just hoped she'd attempt to make progress in it.

Over the course of the next year and a half, I had many wonderful (and often hilarious) chats with my Mama about my transition. I remember one in particular: She was in the kitchen cooking us supper while I was sitting at the bar chatting with her. Somehow, we got on the topic of my transition, and she was trying so hard to understand what I was going through, but it was just so complicated that, in exasperation, she threw her hands up and said, "Why can't you just go back to being a lesbian?!"

The comment was in jest and did not at all mean to do me harm, and when I heard it, I laughed the hardest I'd laughed in so long.

That was probably the moment I realized how much progress Mama had made and was continuing to make. A couple years prior, when I told her I was dating women, she took it so hard that she had to take days off of work, so to hear her say that like it was nothing showed me how far she had come since the day I told her I loved women. It showed me how comfortable she was talking and joking with me—even about serious things. But most importantly, it gave me hope that the way she viewed my life was being re-imagined. She was truly trying to understand me and what my life could end up looking like. It was just hard.

Isn't it always, though? Isn't it always difficult to re-imagine life? We all have dreams for ourselves and for the people we love, and we're constantly having to re-imagine them. It's *always* hard.

I don't have kids yet, but I have dreams for them. I want them to be safe, and I want them to know they're loved, and I want each of them to be a loving and peaceful presence to those around them. I want them to have passions and I want them to chase those passions with all their strength. However, they might be passionate about things I wouldn't normally give a damn about. I can't imagine having a child who doesn't care about sports or music, but the reality is that I might. We come to our own lives and the lives of the people we love with deep-seated expectations. The reality is that we constantly have to re-imagine them because no person will live up to our imagined versions of them; they just won't. Others can't always be who we expect them to be, and thank God for that.

When I realized I was Brett, I had to re-imagine my life: I never expected to experience the struggles of my real name not matching my legal name; I never expected to love women; I never expected to be a voice in the LGBTQ community; but here we are. The more I learn about myself and the more I live into being Brett, the more I have to rethink who I will be and how I will live. Quite frankly, I think it's easier for me to do that than for my family to do that for me. I get to know my own thoughts and dreams as they happen; they don't. It's not their job to hope and dream for me, but it's natural that they do.

So that's what Mama was doing—re-imagining her expectations for me—because "having a transgender son" was never a section heading in her metaphorical parental handbook. It was hard for her, and it was hard for me to see her struggling with it because I just wanted it to all make sense to her the way it all made sense to me. For a while, it just didn't, but she wrestled so well with it, and she always, always, *always* reminded me how much she loved me and that she would never turn her back on me.

Even before she was able to call me Brett, it was her love that repeatedly assured me I could live and live well as Brett.

The E-mail

My family did a really good job of making sure that I didn't have to come out to every single family member on my own. My Mama told her parents and sister's family, and my grandparents passed on the information to the extended family members who needed to know. To this day, I have no idea how my Dad's side of the family found out because I didn't tell them, but I know they know. I was really appreciative of the effort my family put in; it would have been so exhausting and painful for me to have that conversation with every single person.

Even though everyone found out around the same time, it was still a long process for them to call me Brett and use male pronouns. They all made their progress at various speeds with various methods of acceptance or lack thereof.

My Grandma was the first person to get on board with my name. It surprised me a little bit because my Grandpa is a pastor, my Grandma is the perfect pastor's wife, and both of them have conservative leanings. But if I ever know how to love people half as well as they do, I will be a wonderful man, so their support wasn't entirely shocking. Grandma was well ahead of the family curve, though. She sent me an e-mail updating me on life at home and she addressed it to Brett. At the very end, she wrote something like this: "You probably noticed I wrote this to Brett. It's been a hard year getting to this place, but I want you to know that I love you and that I'm with you every step of this journey. Calling you Brett is where I'll start." She went on to explain that she began by writing my name in her phone book, in her emails, and in her letters. She hoped that seeing it written everywhere like that would make it easier for her to speak that name naturally and comfortably.

Seeing my name—my real name—written by my Grandma was overwhelmingly beautiful and exciting. Even though I had known I was Brett for a year, seeing the tangible ways in which my Grandma was coming alongside me made a world of difference. Shortly after my Grandma's email, I received one from my Mama with very similar words. Grandma came up with the idea, and Mama thought it was a good one.

But the time between when my family knew I was Brett and when they actually called me Brett was incredibly awkward. They tried to be as supportive as they could, but they couldn't bring themselves to call me Brett, which meant they tried to refrain from calling me any name or using any pronouns. If you've ever tried to talk to or about someone without names *or* pronouns, you know it's damn near impossible. You pretty much need one or the other. So that led to some awkward moments when no one knew what to say or uncomfortable silences when people knew they had said something wrong. There were times I would leave the room because my family's inability to acknowledge me as anything—a name nor a gender—was unbearable. There were times when hearing my old name was so painful I had to step away. Even though I knew none of my family members wanted to hurt me, and that most of them were trying the hardest they could, their process was still painful for me. It's hard to finally figure out a truth about yourself and realize that you then have to wait for others to figure it out.

Their level of acceptance didn't make my identity as Brett any more true or false, but life is relational; therefore, who I am is, in some ways, wrapped up in the people I love and who the people I love think I am. Most days, that's a good thing because they're often more charitable to me than I am to myself, but it makes the uncomfortable stages of transition all the more difficult.

The men in my family were much slower to accept my name change than were the women. For part of that time, I didn't speak to some of them because it was just too much for me. This is a long and complicated part of my story that has not yet been resolved. There has not been the necessary acknowledgment of wrongs, nor have we exchanged apologies. While this is an important part of my story—a part rich in life lessons—this is a place that I cannot explore publicly...at least not until the necessary reparations have been made. What I will say is this: the road to acceptance of a new name is not easy—not for a trans person and not for a trans person's family. It is, however, easy to create deep wounds (on both sides), and those wounds will stay wounds until people put the energy and effort into bandaging them up. For me, that has yet to happen.

What has happened, though, is I now have a family that always calls me Brett and uses male pronouns in reference to me. I have a Mama who tells me how hard it is to remember what life was like before I was Brett—before I was myself. I have grandparents who go to bat for me and are never, ever ashamed that I am their grandkid. I have cousins who still love to spend time with me and say things like, "Thank you, sir." They don't have to gender me that way, but they choose to because they know me and they know I love that. I have an Aunt and Uncle who tell me they are so proud I'm their nephew.

I have a family that calls me by my name.

I have a family who knows *I am Brett* and love me *for* it, not in spite of it.

On Embodiment

Names are more than just words that describe us; they are foundational to our being. Names encompass our whole selves in a way that mere descriptors don't. I could call you pretty or smart, but that's not who you are. Those words are just parts of your existence. But your name—Layne, Alex, Matt, Lacey, Lizzie, Mark, Drew, Pam—is who you are. Our names, in their fullest form, are embodied. I would be remiss to talk about becoming Brett without also talking about the physical transitions my body has made.

Before I get into the specifics of the physical journey I have taken, it's important to reiterate that my story is not the story of every trans person. We are a very broad and diverse community of people. What it means for me to be a trans person—particularly with respect to the way I relate to my body—might be totally different than what it means to your trans friend.

Some trans people want to have every surgery available, and they want to be on hormones for the rest of their lives. Others don't want any surgeries, but they want to be on hormones for a short time. Some don't want to do any type of physical transition. Still others opt for other combinations of these options. There is nothing wrong with any of these routes. There is no "right" way to be trans. And the important thing is not the path we take but that we are following the one that makes us fully ourselves. This is not a map of the journey of every trans person with a trans body; this is simply the way I relate to my body. This is the story of a boy who finally fell in love with himself—nothing more, and nothing less.

By the time I was willing to admit to others that I was trans, I knew it to be true so deeply that I was ready to hit the ground running. I knew beyond a shadow of a doubt that I was Brett, so I knew I couldn't spend a single second longer living as anybody else. I knew I was going to go on hormones, and I knew I'd at least have top surgery. In fact, I wanted all of those things to happen immediately. Patience was a virtue that lived thousands of miles from my grip.

But neither of these things could happen until I told my family. Because of that, I fell back on my roots as a person who loved to do research. I researched everything because I liked to know as much as possible about everything I might ever want to talk about and because I liked being 100% confident in the decisions I made. When I couldn't actually transition, then, I researched everything about transitioning. I researched surgeries and hormones and doctors. I watched videos of peoples' transition stories — the good ones and the horror stories. I made phone calls to various medical centers and gender studies professors all across the state. Within a few months, I could tell you almost everything about a physical transition that the internet could supply.

Unfortunately, among the information I gathered was the fact that my insurance wouldn't pay for any part of my transition—not even the preliminary blood work to see if it would be safe for me to start hormones. You wouldn't think blood work would be terribly expensive, but that alone was almost $600. Transitioning is not cheap. Also among the information I scrounged up on the internet was the far cheaper, yet far more dangerous, testosterone black market. For once in my life, I did the smart and responsible thing and refused to become a part of that scene. I'm sure my body and my loved ones will continue to thank me for that.

Anyway, at that time, I was working a part-time job at a local Panera Bread. I worked a lot of hours for little pay, but I knew I had to do something to make money if I ever wanted to be able to transition. I think it was March of 2012—six months after I had my revelation and three months after I admitted it to my parents—when I no longer had the ability to wait for hormone replacement therapy. I sent an e-mail to my parents. I broke down the cost of testosterone. I explained that it would be safe, that I would be able to pay for the testosterone itself — just not the blood work up front. I assured them if they lent me $300, I would pay them back in full within two months. I think I might have even offered to pay interest. In response to the e-mail, I received a text asking if they could call me. Right after I got off work, I sat in my car in the parking garage and I called them. The yellow-tinted, empty garage that housed that conversation is still sketched clearly in my mind.

The talk did not go well. They thought it was far too soon for me to be making that kind of decision. What if I regretted it? What if I realized I was wrong and I wanted to go back when the damage had already been done? The moment I heard those words, I began crying. I sobbed and I yelled at my Mama. I told her she wasn't listening and that she didn't get it. She didn't understand that I couldn't live the way I was living any longer and that once I started physically transitioning, I'd never want to go back. She apologized and agreed that she didn't get it. I told her to forget about it. Then, I hung up.

For a long, long time I sat in my car and beat up the steering wheel. I felt so far away from myself—like I would never be able to simply be who I was. The best way I can think to describe the kind of dysphoria I was feeling was this completely overwhelming desire to rip myself out of my own body. The only worse thing I've experienced is the continual realization that ripping yourself out of your body is impossible.

The next few months passed slowly and my mind stayed ever on hormones and top surgery. The hormones felt more immediately necessary than top surgery. Perhaps it was because, realistically, I knew that the cost of top surgery put it much further out in my future than hormones could be. Also helpful in curbing my need for top surgery was finding a well-fitting binder. A binder is a very tight undershirt, for lack of a better word; its sole purpose is to flatten a chest. Once I found a successful binder, I was able to pass as a male a lot more frequently—though normally as a twelve-year-old boy. Even that little binder meant something huge for me. It was the most uncomfortable thing I'd ever put on my body, but it was the first thing that made me feel any semblance of comfort existing in my own body since the day I realized I am trans.

But I couldn't do anything on my own about the fact that my voice was octaves too high. There was nothing I could do on my own to get the five o'clock shadow, which I so desperately wanted, to cross my face. Testosterone was the only thing that could make those changes a reality. And I *needed* them to be a reality. That necessity is something I think only trans people *really* understand. I mean, a cisgender person can understand what a "need" is, obviously, and I think they can be sympathetic to our struggle, but the only way to really understand what it means to *need* these types of changes is to be a trans person who feels like they need them. Some people describe this as feeling like we're in the wrong body, but that wasn't my experience. It was never so much feeling trapped in the wrong body as it was feeling that my body just wasn't the way it was supposed to be. My body has always felt like it belonged to me; like it made me...me. It's just been a body that has needed to make a transition to be fully itself — to make me fully myself. And it was so incredibly frustrating to finally figure out the kind of transition I needed to make and to not be able to do it.

Throughout the summer of 2012, I worked my ass off. I needed testosterone. I didn't know how much longer I could live without it without going crazy. I saved up some money, but, admittedly, it wasn't much. By fall, I had almost enough money saved up for my blood work, but if I had used it, I would have had nothing in my savings account, which meant I wouldn't have even been able to afford the testosterone once I had the blood work done. I remember talking to my girlfriend at the time and to my best friend about how I just didn't know what to do. I was at a loss for how to get the money I needed because I knew I couldn't ask my family. I was also scared of what would happen if I started the hormones without talking to my family again. I was scared to move forward and I was scared to stay where I was. But my friends gave great advice. They told me I ought to ask all of my friends for a little help.

We as a country, I think, have a stigma about asking for financial assistance. We don't want to do it. For some reason, it's perfectly acceptable to ask a friend to help you through life's hardest times in any way...except for in a monetary fashion. It's like we hold our friends close but our money closer. But they told me not to fall into that trap. They reminded me that I had a great community of friends around me, friends who would be more than happy to help me out. It probably took them about a month to coax me into making a fundraising page. I was so uncomfortable with asking for help. I felt ashamed. I felt like I was a failure for not being able to afford my life on my own. I felt like people were judging me. And I'm sure some of them were, but I doubt anyone was judging me as hard as I was judging myself. I refused to simply accept donations; in exchange for their money, I wrote letters, or I recorded CDs, or I made poetry books. I even had a living room concert for the highest donor. My friends convinced me that if I did that, people would be paying me for my art. I wish, though, that I didn't have to make myself feel ashamed to just ask for help. (Don't we all?)

In a matter of a few days, I had more than enough money to cover the entire cost of my blood work and my first month of testosterone. My friends and friends of my friends really showed me that they had my back. That December, I was able to start on testosterone, and I've never looked back.

Doctors use various methods to start patients on testosterone. The most common method is to start with a small dose and work your way up to a maintenance dose. My doctor was not a common doctor. From day one, she had me on a weekly maintenance dose. There's nothing technically wrong this, but, and I don't know if you know this or not, hormones control a lot of shit in our bodies. They control our appetite (sexual and otherwise), they affect our moods and our anxieties, and they affect our level of hydration; they control so much. To put a high amount of testosterone into a completely unaware body can—and for me, did—cause some problems.

For starters, I was starving. Constantly. There was hardly ever a time, especially on my shot days (these hormones are injected), that I didn't want to eat an entire large pizza. I also constantly wanted to have sex. My friends might tell you that was nothing new, but believe me, it was way different than anything I'd experienced before. The most noticeable and unfortunate differences, though, were in my hydration and my anxiety. I've never done a great job keeping myself appropriately hydrated—I much prefer Coke to water—but I'd never dealt with dehydration quite like that before. My doctor warned me that testosterone would dehydrate me, but I wasn't smart enough to figure out that that meant I needed to drastically increase my intake of water. So I was struck with massive cramps all the time. When I say massive, I mean, limbs-curling-up-uncontrollably-massive. And when I say all the time, I mean multiple times a day, even when I wasn't doing anything that warranted a cramp. It was a horrible way to live for a few weeks. I didn't understand what was happening, but I eventually figured out that if I just drank more water, the cramps would go away.

The anxiety, on the other hand, was not a simple fix. Again, my doctor was kind enough to warn me that my anxiety might increase when I went on testosterone, but I didn't really trust her. I should have. It didn't exactly increase, but my anxiety changed. Before testosterone, my anxiety presented itself in sweaty palms and upset stomachs, but after testosterone, it presented itself in full-blown panic attacks. It presented itself in a convulsing body and a racing heart. Every time I had a panic attack, there were small parts of me that literally thought I was dying; it felt how I imagined a heart attack would feel every time.

But it was worth it. There has never been a single second of my life since I started testosterone that I've wondered if it was worth it. I remember the night I convulsed for three hours in my parents' bed (they were concerned about me falling out of my own and hurting myself) and even in the midst of that, I never questioned whether it was worth it. They questioned it. Others questioned it. But to me, it was always worth it. Even with that kind of anxiety, I was infinitely more myself, and I knew that from the moment I was stuck with my very first shot.

One of the biggest joys of the hormones was being able to document the changes it made in me — both mentally and physically. I captured my vocal changes through recording songs. It was wild how quickly my voice dropped. And every day I recorded a message to myself because I wanted to be able to hear exactly how and when it dropped. Some days it seemed to drop miles, and other days it felt like it was reverting. The voice cracks during this phase of my transition warranted many laughs from my friends and me.

The most significant thing about testosterone for me was that it caused me to be interested in my body in a non-hateful way for the first time. I liked to see how the hair on my legs grew and watch as random hairs sprouted on my face. I liked to see how my hairline changed. I liked to see how my arms got thicker. I liked knowing my body. It wasn't exactly the way I wanted it yet, and there were certainly still plenty of days when looking in the mirror caused dysphoria, but for the most part, I had a healthy fascination with myself that I'd never had before.

I knew, though, that I'd never be totally okay in my body unless I had top surgery; I knew that it was a necessity for me. In the spring of 2014, I went through a serious break-up. And when I called to tell my Mama, and she asked what happened, I had to admit that it was in large part due to the way I was struggling with depression again. She said all the right words during that phone call, and she assured me that it was going to be okay. I think hearing me talk about my depression really got her thinking, because a few days later, I got a text, completely out of the blue, that said, "Have you thought about having top surgery this summer?" (Keep in mind that years had passed between my call to her for help with testosterone and her offer to help with top surgery — years that had produced much growth and acceptance in her.) I told her I thought about having top surgery every day, but that I'd never be able to afford it by the summer. She asked if I thought it would make me happier and if it could help with my anxiety and depression. I told her I didn't know about the latter, but that it would definitely make me happier. She told me to call the doctor and make the necessary appointments; she'd pay for the surgery and I could pay her back when I had a full-time job. I had to ask her five times if she was serious; it's an expensive (at least $7,000) surgery, and I didn't want to get my hopes up if she changed her mind. She promised she meant it.

I made some calls and found a doctor in Omaha, Nebraska that had done one of my friends' surgeries. We made the decision to go forward with top surgery in late May, and on July 3, 2014, I went to Omaha with my Mama and her parents for the surgery. My plan was to be home by July 4 to catch some fireworks. I was eager for us to get back home so we could celebrate the 4th with Mama's partner and my new body for the first time. My grandparents and my Mama knew better than that, though. They kept reminding me that this was a major surgery and that I shouldn't get my hopes up about being able to do a lot right away. I thought they were underestimating my recovery abilities.

It turns out, friends, that top surgery *is*, in fact, a major surgery. The day after, I could hardly get out of the hotel bed, let alone spend four hours in a car driving home. And there was absolutely no way I was going out anywhere to watch fireworks. I spent my first real day of freedom in a hotel room with my closest family members watching distant fireworks through a window. It was the best day of liberation I've ever had—my own independence day.

I'm lucky. I'm lucky that surgery was a possibility for me. And I'm even luckier that my family was supportive enough to come with me. The staff in the surgical center commented over and over again how great it was to see that I had so many family members with me to take care of me. Apparently, and unfortunately, that's a rarity.

The weeks after surgery were hard. I had to rely on others so much more than I was used to because I was sick from the pain medicine, I was in pain despite the medicine, and I couldn't use my arms to do much at all. I couldn't lift any weight; I couldn't push or pull anything; I couldn't even open my own car door. We had to move everything I might possibly want down from the cabinets onto the countertops so I could reach them. It was hard, but I had great people taking great care of me. I'm a needy little patient, but if I wanted a Reese's, Mama's partner went out and got me a Reese's. If I wanted a malt, my Mama made me a malt. When I needed a popsicle, or my drains emptied, or my bandages changed, my Mama took care of me. I am so very lucky.

The surgery didn't make everything perfect right away. The healing was hard. It took a long time before I could sleep laying down. It took even longer before I was comfortable. My stitches made me want to throw up every time I looked at them and I feared that when my stitches were gone, my scars would do the same. For a while, they did. For a while I'd look at my chest and I'd think, "I love this, I love the way this feels, but I can never let anyone see it." I was ashamed of those scars. There was still a part of me that thought real men didn't have those scars on their chests.

But then I got my head out of my ass and realized how beautiful I was. It was late one night a few weeks after my surgery. I was sleeping on the recliner in the living room because I still couldn't lie down flat. But this night, I was wide awake and I had the urge to write. So I picked up a pen and paper and I just started pouring my feelings onto the page. What came out was the poem that appeared at the beginning of this book.

I wrote those words and I realized that I meant them. I realized that for the first time in my life I could, without a doubt, say that I loved myself. I realized that the scars on my chest didn't make me any less of a man; they just told the story of how I got to myself. And damn it, it's a long, complicated story, but it's one that I was, and am, so very proud of. The scars on my chest are survival scars; I am forever thankful for their existence. I love that I can touch them and know where I've been and how I got to where I am. I love that when my partner rests her hand on them and tells me she loves me, I can finally believe that she's telling the truth; I can finally believe that yes, someone else can love me as I am, too.

About a week ago—it's the summer of 2015—I saw myself in the mirror getting out of the shower and I did a double take. I tilted my head to the side and I looked at myself. I looked in the mirror, and for the first time I *saw* myself. I saw the body that I had and I was able to say, "That's me." It wasn't this body that is in transition to the body I want. It wasn't this body that I wished *wasn't* my body. It was me. My face looked like me. My eyes looked like me. My hair looked like me. My chest looked like me. And I'm not muscular, or really all that fit, but I looked at myself and I was confident in myself. I said aloud, "Whoa." And when I did, I heard a voice that sounded like mine.

Today I'm sitting at what I believe is the end of my physical transition, and I'm happy, proud, and thankful. I'm happy to finally be at rest within myself. Trans or not, I think being at rest within oneself is quite an accomplishment. I'm proud that I didn't shy away from doing what I knew I had to do to make my body into itself. But most importantly, I'm thankful for all of the people who made and make being myself possible. I literally couldn't have done it without the support—money, hugs, kind words, nice letters, kisses, et cetera—of my family and friends. I couldn't have done it without others believing in me and giving me a safe space to exist.

I'm a man who is able to be my fullest self because the people around me gave me the space to learn how to be at peace with myself. And when I figured out how to do that, they walked with me.

I hope I can be that kind of presence in the lives of those around me.

Chapter Three

The Transitioning Point

My name is important to me because it gives people a way to talk to me that shows they see me as the person I am. It's not that they see me as I hope them to because sometimes they see even more of who I *actually* am than I wish they would. Sometimes authenticity is horrifying. But having people know my name isn't the most important part of my story. The most important part is what I've learned since I've been able to name myself.

I realize that knowing my own name has carried the most weight in my life story. Until I knew my own name, I was completely unable to name the big truths—good and bad—about myself; I was unable to be honest with myself. I couldn't name my passions, the parts of myself that I loved, or the parts of myself that I wished weren't real until I truly knew how to name myself.

I've spent years deliberating over why this is the case. Why was naming myself Brett the key to understanding so much about myself? I'm confident that this question will be on my mind for many years to come, and I'm sure that my list of answers will inevitably get longer. But for now, I propose three reasons.

First, having a name that I love and that attempts to capture the person that I am makes me feel worthy. Before I was able to see that it was wrong for me to live life as someone I am not, I was unable and unwilling to truly name much else about myself. And why would I? If the most fundamental thing about myself—my name— wasn't correct, then why would I spend the time making sure anything else was?

Choosing my name, then, was an act of radical self-love. I had never before done something so loving for myself. When I picked my name, I decided that instead of calling myself the name I was given without question—the name that always made me feel uncomfortable and unloved—I would take the more difficult, true path. In choosing my name, I decided that my happiness and self-care were worth the effort; I decided this task was worth the hard work because *I* am worth the hard work that it takes to have a happy and healthy life. Before naming myself Brett, I didn't believe that; life was always just a treacherous road, and I was unable to imagine it any other way.

But having a name that I loved hearing come out of my mouth and seeing written on my papers gave me hope. I was hopeful that if I could love the way I talked about myself—if I could feel good about it whenever someone addressed me—then maybe things would be okay. Maybe then I could have a good and enjoyable life.

Second, by naming myself Brett, I was able to see who truly supported and loved me. Calling someone a new name and using different gender identifiers is not an easy task. While I understand that it *should* be commonplace for people to be more than happy to walk alongside their transgender loved ones, I know that's not the case. I know this world doesn't make it easy for trans people or our allies. So the fact that people chose to walk alongside me is no small thing. It takes a great deal of commitment for my loved ones to say they will not turn away from me; they will not stop loving me even if it means their lives will become more difficult as mine does.

Finding that kind of support was crucial for being able to identify the truths about myself. It's not that they had done anything in the past to suggest that they didn't support me, but when everything about myself felt fake to me, it was hard to believe their support was real. Their love and support became real to me when they chose to walk with me on my journey when they could have turned away. Once I believed that they really did care about and support me, I was free to be honest with myself and with them because I didn't have fear that they would all abandon me if they truly knew me.

To some extent, though, that fear has stuck with me. During months of depression, my best friends have to remind me that they're not going anywhere. They remind me often that they still like and love me. But now I'm comfortable telling them when I need to hear that affirmation, and I'm confident (at least rationally) that they won't actually leave. That kind of confidence and trust has spurred my ability to get to know who I am and to actually be that person.

Third, there comes a point at which the truth, no matter how difficult, is better to live into than continuing to live in secret. For me, that point came when I realized I was Brett. Through previous months of AA, I was growing more and more honest with myself and with others. The life of an honest person was far more enjoyable than the life of a secret-keeper. The "Brett secret" was far too large for me to keep — so large that once I told people, I thought nothing else had the potential to be as divisive as that. Once I told people and realized that I *would* still have a family, friends, romantic interests, and a place in my church, I also realized that I no longer needed to keep any secrets. Sharing the truth of my real name was so liberating that I had no choice but to keep telling the truth about myself. I didn't know how not to; I didn't know how else to live.

Before I could tell others the truth about myself, though, I had to know it. I quickly realized after naming myself Brett that even though I used to think I knew myself incredibly well, I was a complete mystery. For example, I used to think I was extremely extroverted. Anyone who knows me now is laughing at that statement. I was never extroverted—I simply thought extroversion was synonymous with being a loud drunk.

But once I knew myself as Brett—and once my brain had squeezed out all the vodka—I quickly began to figure other things out. What follows in the rest of this book is an exploration of some of the truths that I've been able to identify about myself. These truths are central to the man I am today. Since the day I gave myself a name of love and acceptance, I have taken responsibility for the task of identifying the important parts of myself that need love and acceptance, too.

On Being a Man

When I realized I was a man, I quickly learned that I had no idea what it meant to be a man. It was a strange feeling. I thought it would be simple; I thought that if I told people I was a man, I would know how to be a man, and that — as they say — would be that. But my experience was quite different.

Being a man comes with a lot of conditions that I didn't expect. They started pouring in just after I had told people that I was Brett and before I had started any sort of medical transition. It was as if the people around me expected me to immediately make huge changes in the way I lived. People started making suggestions for how I should alter the way I walked and talked. They told me to hold open more doors for women. And they told me I had better start paying when I went out on dates. They didn't want me to love watching Pretty Little

Liars or Gossip Girl. Making all of these changes, they said, would make me more of a man.

At first, I listened to them. I searched YouTube for video after video of trans men teaching other trans men how to "pass." (To "pass" means, in this case, "to pass as a man." Many trans people give advice to others about how to "pass" so that people don't question their gender identities.) I watched videos that told me to make sure my voice inflection was more flat-lined than it used to be. They taught me how to walk manly, and I spent more time than I'd care to admit practicing that new walk in the mirror. They taught me how to take up more space in a room or a crowd — because men generally take up more space than women do. I learned to sit with my legs opened instead of crossed and to keep my shoulders back to make them appear broader.

Learning to pass was an obsession of mine. It wasn't long before I started to fit the bill of a heterosexual cisgender man. The problem was that Brett was not and is not a heterosexual cisgender man. Brett is a transgender man with a queer sexuality. Even though I was living as Brett, I was a long way from confidently *living into* who Brett was.

There were other pressures, too. People say men have low voices and don't have boobs, but I was at my manliest back when my chest and voice signified femininity. (I just have to say, some of the best men I know have voices that are much higher and chests that are much larger than mine.) But when given a clear picture of what a man is — a hairy person with a flat chest and a deep voice — what's a guy like me to do? It was impossible for my physical specifications to match that at the time, so I threw myself into matching every other aspect of manliness that I could with full force.

The whole point of becoming Brett was so that I could be myself, but when I realized what people wanted men to be, I promptly turned my back on myself again. I was afraid that if I didn't fit the manly mold, no one would ever think I was the man I knew I was.

So I opened doors and I paid for dates. I was crude and I smoked too much. I did whatever I could to make it easier and more "natural" for others to see that I was a man. And I did that for a long time. But I couldn't shake off the calling to be myself. It followed my every move. That saying, "Wherever you go, there you are," had never been truer for me. I couldn't escape from myself into some person that was more palatable. That's not the way it works.

I can't tell you the moment I gave the middle finger to the standards of what makes a man. Maybe there wasn't a single moment; more than likely, it was a long, slow process. That's how most things in my life work. What I can tell you is that it took until the early winter of 2014 for me to really begin to be okay with it.

In the winter of 2014 I found myself nearing the end of my first semester at Duke Divinity School in Durham, North Carolina. I had a love-hate relationship with starting school at Duke. I loved it because it meant I got to study theology with some of the most fascinating people in the world. I also loved it because it meant I got to live by my best friends again after having lived across the country from them for a year. I hated it, though, because I had no idea what I wanted to do with my life. I often questioned whether I was in the right degree path. And, to be real, who wants to spend tens of thousands of dollars on a degree if it might not be the degree they need for their future career?

My best friend is really the important factor in this story. I have never been so irrevocably and covenantally committed to another person as I am to him. I love him for who he is, and he loves me for who I am. We tell each other everything; I'm sure some people say we tell each other too much. We joke around constantly, but we also talk about all of the serious stuff that we're too ashamed to tell anyone else. And we're always there to remind each other that, even in those times, we are still brothers and we always will be.

In the winter of 2014 I became more fully aware that I am attracted to all kinds of people—women, of course, but also men and genderqueer people. It was surprising to me how hard of a pill that was to swallow. I've loved and accepted the LGBTQ community ever since I knew what it was, and by 2014, I was incredibly proud to be a trans man. But it was still unfortunately difficult for me to confidently admit that I wasn't a heterosexual trans man. There's a strange expectation that to be a good man is to be a heterosexual, manly-man who chases after women all of his life. I've never quite had the manly-man part down, but I've done a hell of a lot of chasing women and I feared that if the scope of my attraction went beyond that, people would again begin questioning whether or not I was a real man. I wasn't ready to go through that questioning again.

Until that winter, I made a lot of gay jokes, usually behind closed doors, and I thought it was okay because I was a part of the queer community. But one day, my best friend and I were talking about why I did that, and I just realized it was because I was hiding something. Making gay jokes was a self- and community-deprecating way of identifying another truth about myself. It wasn't healthy and it wasn't kind, and I'm so grateful that I had someone to remind me that an attraction to men doesn't make me any less of a real man. It blows my mind that I could be immersed in the queer community for so long and still have such a backward expectation of sexuality for myself.

As I came to terms with the fact that my understanding of sexuality and being a "real" man was ridiculously skewed, I started to wonder what else about my perception of my gender was distorted. You see, I wasn't always afraid that my sexuality would make people think I was less of a man. That had come about during my years of transition. Every single one of us gets socialized in some way or another based on the genders we present. What I wasn't aware of until I realized my fear about my sexuality was that during my years of transition, I had been re-socialized in ways I wasn't proud of.

My years of seeking out people to teach me what it means to be a man were both helpful and harmful. They were helpful because I was able to blend in before I had started any sort of physical transition. I was able to use the men's restroom because they taught me how men generally behave in the bathroom. They helped me learn how men carried themselves so that I wouldn't stick out. I was so grateful to the men in my life who taught me what it meant to them to be "manly." The fact that they would take the time to teach me all they knew felt like they were welcoming me into their club. It felt like they believed I was a man and they wanted me to have the life of a man just like they did; they wanted me to be like them. It was a great feeling, and it was helpful at first. Because of what they taught me, I fit in with men in a way that was incredibly refreshing; I fit in with men in a way that I had never really fit in anywhere before. That type of acceptance lessened the social anxiety that I had always struggled with.

I don't think there is any fundamental problem with this kind of education and acceptance. There are aspects of it that I have carried with me for years and will continue to carry with me. For example, my theology professor taught me about how much respect a man gets when he ties his own bow ties. So I bought some bow ties and learned to tie them myself. This is not to say that every man needs to wear bow ties or that there's any shame in not tying your own; I mean to say that some of the things I learned during my re-socialization, including tying my own bow tie, really resonated with me and made me more myself. And I feel my best in a good-looking, well-tied bow tie.

However, some of the re-socialization I went through didn't make me feel like myself; some of what I did in attempt to be a "real" man carried me further away from the man I really was. In certain ways, many men behave in ways that are distinct from many women or genderqueer individuals. I don't think there's anything particularly wrong with those types of generalizations. The problem comes when we assume that people who don't fit those generalizations are somehow less manly. The problem comes when we give up on ourselves in order to play the "ideal" man role as it was presented to us. The reality is this: if we don't naturally fit into the "ideal" man or woman, then it's not really ideal for us.

When my best friend affirmed that I was a man no matter my sexuality, I finally felt free from the expectations that others had imposed on my sense of manhood—and expectations I had imposed on myself. I began sitting with my legs crossed again and talking with my hands. I let my voice go wherever it chose to go when I spoke. I embraced my love of candles. I continued to tie my own bow ties and to talk way too much about sports. I continued to burp at times when my Mama would tell me to mind my manners, and I still hold doors open for people. I finally started letting myself talk about feelings and cry when I felt like crying. I started telling people I loved them more often, and I became unafraid to give my friends—even my male friends—kisses on the cheek when we parted ways. I stopped fearing whether or not onlookers would think I was gay or not man enough, and I just let me be me.

Of course, I recognize that the ability to do this—
to be myself—comes to me partly because of how
privileged I am. First, I am incredibly privileged to
have people, especially my best friend, who love
me enough to be committed to me as I sort
through my gender expectations and explorations.
There are so many trans people who don't have
communities like that. I don't know about them,
but I know that I couldn't be myself without my
best friend and everyone who puts up with my
incessant gender questions and experiments. It's a
privilege to have that kind of support. It's also a
privilege to have had top surgery and to have
been on testosterone for years. Truthfully, both of
those things make it easier to feel free as myself.
Fewer people will question if I'm a man—even if
I'm in touch with my feminine side—simply
because I have a flat chest and facial hair.

I'm privileged, and that privilege is necessary for
me to feel comfortable living as I am. But it

shouldn't be that way. I didn't go on testosterone or have my top surgery to appease the people who think a deep voice and flat chest qualify someone as a man; I did it because that's who I am. But there are many trans men who don't want to go on testosterone or have surgery, and many more who, for one reason or another, do not have access to that kind of medical care. They are no less manly than myself, and we have to start recognizing that.

I truly believe the only way we will begin to save and care for the lives of trans men is by changing the language we use to talk about masculinity. Only when we stop assuming that all men should have penises and present themselves in particular ways will we even begin to care for the lives of trans men as much as we should. And that's also the way we will start caring for cisgender men the way we should. Not all cisgender men align well with the male gender expectations, either.

I can't count the number of times I've talked to men who are too afraid to tell their friends they love them because they don't want people to think they're gay; or men who are afraid to cry in front of anyone else because they don't want to be perceived as weak; or men who won't let their kids paint their nails because they don't want to be seen as womanly. And these men wish that they could do all of these things, but the expectations on their masculinity are so high that they just can't cross that threshold.

Shying away from who we are because who we are doesn't meet some arbitrary ideal is no way to live. We do a disservice to those around us by not being ourselves. We might think we want to be a specific kind of man, but communities only flourish when we let people be who they are.

Therefore, the first thing I learned once I knew I was a man was that I had no idea what it meant to be a man, but one of the most important things I realized was that I didn't have to know.

I just had to be myself.

The Humor

During my "be a manly man" phase, I experienced a lot of failure. That's what happens every time I try to be someone I'm not: I fail. The same professor who taught me about bow ties, though, also taught me a great deal about how to handle failure. I don't know if he knew that was what he was doing every time he poked fun at me, but he was.

I had (and still have) a great relationship with that man. For some reason, one I cannot wrap my head around, a lot of students are afraid of him—probably because they hear he's a tough grader. So I remember one of my first weeks at school when I made some smartass comment to him and he said, "Hey, you're a freshman, you're supposed to be scared of me." I responded with something like, "Well, I'm not, so I guess you'd better get scarier." We looked each other in the eye for bit after that and then both started laughing. I knew we would have a good relationship going forward.

Don't get me wrong, there were times he was disappointed in my work, and there were times I thought he was unfair. There were times he thought I was slacking off when I was doing all that I could do. But he was the first person to tell me I was smart and that if theology was what I wanted to do, I could do it alongside the best in the field; he was the first person whose compliments I was able to let sink in. He was the first person to help me grow in confidence in my brain's abilities to carry me through the world. The confidence and support he constantly showed me—even when he showed it to me through tough love—was the only way I made it through my undergrad experience and into Duke.

He and I still talk regularly; in fact, just the other day we were talking about how I came out to him as a trans man. Neither of us could remember how that conversation happened. It must not have been earth-shaking or life-changing for either of us, and I'm pretty okay with that. My coming out to him wasn't that significant, but the way he interacted with me afterward was.

He has a habit of calling most of his students by their last names. I'm not sure when or why that started, but it's something he's known for. That means he never really called me Bri, so when I told him my name was actually Brett, he asked if he could still just call me by my last name. I was perfectly fine with that; it was nice to have some sort of consistency amid the transition everywhere else. He warned me that he would make mistakes with pronouns, and he did make them, just like almost everyone else. The way he handled his mistakes and classmates' mistakes, though, was radically different than the way many other people handled theirs.

When people who genuinely want to be supportive of me make name or pronoun mistakes, a whirlwind of apologies and feelings usually follow. Typically, they feel awful about messing up, and they want to make it known over and over again about how sorry they are. I appreciate the sentiment, but honestly, it's so much more awkward to be repeatedly apologized to than to just move on.

I think he knew this intuitively, so when he made mistakes, or if he was around when others made mistakes, instead of drawing it out, he just made little jokes. He and I picked on each other constantly before my transition, so that this type of relationship continued through my transition was natural. He would make jokes about me going through puberty again, and when my voice cracked, he wasn't afraid to laugh with me. When I would get in trouble with any of the many girlfriends I cycled through throughout undergrad, he would always blame it on the new hormones running through my body.

He was the man I went to most frequently with questions about how to be a man. This was partly because he was the only man I knew I could trust with those conversations, but mostly, it was because he was the kind of man I wanted to be. Sometimes he'd give me advice and I'd try it out and it just wouldn't work for me. Afterward, we'd joke about my often hilarious failures.

This method — this type of joking around — wouldn't work for everyone. For some trans men, this kind of relationship would be way too intense and the joking wouldn't be well received. I'm confident, though, that my professor knows how to read a room; he wouldn't have behaved the way he did if he didn't know I would be more than able to take it. And I appreciated him for it.

I had taken myself so damn seriously for so long, and I needed someone like him to add a little laughter to my life. It's hard not to take a transition really seriously; it's a serious matter. But I'm a perfectionist, and transitioning is messy. There aren't any clean lines or a crisp map, and nothing works out perfectly the way we expect it to. The humor that my relationship with my professor added during my transition experience helped me learn to accept the messiness of the transition — of life in general. I would have gone crazy without it.

Before I was Brett, I had detailed plans for my life. I held great expectations of where I would go and exactly when I would get there. But that's not the way life works, and I didn't know how to deal with that. I didn't know how to handle the twists and turns. I didn't know how to take life in stride when its stride wasn't in sync with mine.

But laughing through every voice crack and goofy failure made me lighten up. Living as Brett is a much lighter experience than anything I've ever experienced before. There is so much liberation in being able to laugh at myself. I can breathe easier when I no longer pack the mistakes and failures into the heavy baggage I carry on my shoulders; instead, I laugh at inside jokes and take to heart lessons I can look back on with minimal pain.

It might seem ridiculous to dedicate pages of this book to humor, but I'm convinced that humor has saved my life. Once I became Brett and was freed to stop taking myself so seriously, I was able to start taking risks again. And taking risks means to have fun again. I recently spent a week with the groom's people for my roommate's wedding, which meant spending two days of my life dancing—in public! Before becoming Brett, I never would have been able to do that. I would have sat at the table, rooted there in fear of looking stupid, and watched everyone else have fun.

But that's not who I am anymore. My professor was an important element of my formation because he taught me to throw myself into life. He taught me that if I go all-in, I'm bound to look like a fool sometimes (and I definitely look like a fool on the dance floor). But part of the joy of life is laughing about your own foolishness with your loved ones.

So much of my newfound joy has been in my ability to laugh with my loved ones. Sometimes laughter comes at my expense, and honestly, I think that's good. It keeps me humble and it reminds me that nothing is as big of a deal as I often try to make it. I never would have realized that life is worth laughing at had I not become Brett. If I hadn't jumped into the deep end of the messy and complicated journey of becoming myself, I never would have found the immense joy that exists in the laughter I share with my friends and, yes — even to this day, with one of my favorite professors.

The Mental Health

Being able to laugh at myself and joke around with my friends has changed life for me, but it hasn't changed everything about me. I'm still the boy who goes through seasons of depression; I'm the boy who has such social anxiety that I plan meals around events that I know will make me so anxious that I have to spend the entire evening that follows hunched over a toilet. The laughter and jokes help, but I'm still me.

Depression and anxiety have chased me through every season of my life. When I was a kid, it mostly centered itself on sports. I've always been competitive, but I would get so nervous about holding my own with the other kids—even if I knew, rationally, that I could. When I played traveling basketball, my coaches always wanted me to be the starting point guard, but I always told them no. There was something about standing on the court in front of everyone just before the jump ball that sent my stomach lurching. At the time, I found no words to make sense of my aversion to being a starting player. It was supposed to be an honor, but now I see that my anxiety was making its debut in my churning stomach.

When I was a swimmer, I told the same story. I was okay once I got in the water, but when I stood up on the starting blocks, I felt like all of the eyes in the room were on me. Around that time, I found a lot of comfort in the Greek word "αγαπη." It's one of the words used in the New Testament to describe God's unending and selfless love for humanity. I started writing "αγαπη" on my left wrist so that when I was down on the starting block, I could focus all of my attention on that word and ignore the eyes that I was sure were burrowing into me. It was quite helpful—so helpful, in fact, that I now have it tattooed in that same place. It's still a calming presence for me.

I've always had bad social anxiety, but if it had to do with sports, I could find some way to handle it. I was far too in love with athletics to let it paralyze me. The real problem came my junior year of high school. When I was a swimmer, I specialized in long-distance butterfly. It was hard on my shoulders, so I developed a long-term injury to my right shoulder. By my junior year of high school, I was in excruciating pain. I couldn't swim, I couldn't play my guitar, I couldn't even lie down comfortably. So in a matter of five months, I had my shoulder operated on twice. The surgeries were only moderately successful. I could move my arm and play guitar again, and I could lift light things over my head. But from that first operation on, I would never be able to swim competitively again.

I had spent eight years making a home in the pool and with my teammates, and I knew that our relationships would never be the same after my surgeries. And they weren't. It was no fault of my own or my former teammates. Some of my closest swimming friends stuck around for a couple years, but I mostly had to find new friends.

Finding new friends is really hard for anyone, but for those of us with extreme social anxiety, it can be almost debilitating to meet and befriend new people. Without swimming, I didn't think I had anything to offer anyone. I thought I needed some sort of social lubrication to break my way into a new friend group. It didn't take me long at all to learn that vodka could easily serve as that lubricant.

The first time I picked up the vodka, I had no idea how to put it down. And I didn't want to. With just a little bit of liquor in my body, I felt like I could talk to anyone. I could go to parties and feel comfortable in the large groups of people. I could be vulnerable with people because if it went horribly wrong, I could just blame it on the booze.

But drinking as much as I did made it hard to know myself well enough to truly be vulnerable.

When I drank, I was trying to drink myself happy. And it worked for a while. When I started feeling depressed or anxious, I just drank a bit and everything would be okay. If I drank a bit before I went out with friends, I had the courage to insert myself into conversations, or to make jokes and have fun. I mourn for my young self who thought fun and joy could only come after consuming alcohol.

I went to extreme measures to "manage" my anxiety and depression. With the amount of vodka that I poured into my body, I convinced myself that I was fine; I was oblivious to the state of my mental health. Sometimes, when I got sober enough, I would hear the mess going on in my head. And when I did, I would talk to a few of my mentors—who I thank God for every single day.

But mostly, I just tried not to let myself get that sober.

I never explicitly told my family about my anxiety and depression; I didn't want them to worry. (Which is a sign that I most certainly should have told them. Friends, if there's cause for your family to worry about you, tell them; it's their job to worry and to help you find a way out.) I think they knew that I was an anxious person, but I never told them how much of an issue it was, so I never went to therapy or took anti-anxiety or anti-depression medications.

During my freshman year of college, when my depression was finally bad enough for me to think anti-depressants were necessary, I took a long, hard look at my drinking habits for the first time since I first picked up the bottle. I decided that I needed to take a break from alcohol. I can't remember if there was a specific event that precipitated that decision or not; life was pretty blurry at that point. What I know is that a couple weeks later, I found myself in my first AA meeting.

I was lucky enough to step into my first meeting with dear friends. I told them I was going to stop drinking, at least for a time, and they offered to meet up with me for a dinner to talk about it. I don't remember much of the conversation (notice a common theme here?), but there were some very important words exchanged. They asked me if I thought I had a problem with alcohol. I told them I thought maybe I did, but it's not like I was an addict or anything. After all, there were periods of my life when I could take almost an entire month off! They both immediately started laughing, while I, oblivious, just stared at them. One of them finally caught her breath and said, "You know, a drinker who doesn't have a problem probably wouldn't feel the need to take a month off, let alone brag about the fact that they could actually do it."

I smiled out of realization about the predicament I was in. "You know," I said, "You're probably right." They invited me to go to their favorite AA meeting that Saturday, and even though I was terrified, I said I'd do it.

They picked me up from my apartment that Saturday just like they said they would. I thought about backing out, but since they were my ride, I really couldn't. (A word of advice: if you ever want to make sure someone keeps his plans with you, offer to pick him up. More often than not, it'll work.) Anyway, it was about a thirty minute drive from my house to the meeting—sufficient time for them to explain meeting protocol and for me to get nervous. They assured me I didn't have to talk; if I just sat and really listened, the power of the meeting would do whatever it was supposed to do. They never did tell me what it was supposed to do.

When we got there, it was obvious to everyone that I was a new face. They all introduced themselves to me, shook my hand, and asked about school and how I knew the people who brought me. But they didn't ask me why I was there. They didn't ask me if I was already a friend of Bill or how many drunken regrets it took me to get down those stairs. They didn't even ask if I was drunk at the time. And I was so glad they didn't. I wasn't drunk, but I wouldn't have known how to answer any of those questions. I didn't know what I was doing there, I just didn't know how to do anything else, either.

I sat on their couch and drank the coffee they offered. I listened to twenty-plus people say over and over again how the AA program had worked and was working miracles for them. As I listened, I found myself turned off by the words they said; it sounded so arrogant for them to talk about how successful their program was. I didn't know at the time that this hopeful message was what I needed to hear. The conversation continued around the circle, and when it finally got to me, before I could stop myself, I blurted out, "My name is Bri, and I'm an alcoholic."

And there it was.

The term "alcoholic" had floated around my head before, but never had it dared to cross the threshold of my lips. It lingered in the silence for what felt like a lifetime before it was interrupted by a group of strangers saying, "Hi, Bri."

So I talked to them. I told them it was my first meeting ever, and I shared some of my thoughts on the devotional that was read. I didn't share anything major, but I shared enough to feel vulnerable and to make a connection with the people in the room. At the end of the meeting, they all gave me hugs. They told me they were glad I was there and that people like me help keep them sober. They told me to keep coming back, and I told them I would. That was the first time in a while that I told someone I would do something and actually believed I would.

And I did stick to it. The program suggests a thing called "90 in 90" for newcomers. That is, it suggests that new people go to 90 meetings in their first 90 days of sobriety. Somehow, I managed to do that. I relapsed after my first 30 days, so my 90 in 90 was more like 120 in 120. It's really quite amazing what a person can learn in four months without the interference of booze. In that short time, I found a sponsor and began working through the steps. I quickly learned that what was perhaps even more difficult than putting down my favorite life crutch was being honest in the way my program required me to be.

I couldn't stay sober and keep lying to myself and to others. I couldn't stay sober and keep the dark parts of myself in the shadows. Either the truth had to come into the light, or I'd go back to the bottom of a bottle. It was that simple. And, luckily, with an exceptional sponsor and many hours in great meetings, I learned that rather quickly.

Truth-telling, though, is difficult, painful, messy, and often terrifying—even when you know your life depends on it. From the time I was young, I had problems with vulnerability; I didn't want people to truly know me because I didn't think I was good enough to be known. It was amazing to be in relationship with people who truly wanted to know me—even the parts of myself that I didn't want to see—and to know that they'd still show up every day to support and love me regardless. It was a love I had never before let myself feel. Don't get me wrong, it was not always an easy, enjoyable love. It was a love that required I admit when I screwed up—even if no one else knew what I had done. It was a love that sometimes left people mad and disappointed in me and I in them. But it was the best kind of love in the world. It was the kind of love that transcends time and space. I know I could call any one of them right now, though years have passed since my first meeting and I'm now living states away, and they'd be more than happy to chat with me.

Those honest conversations shaped my life as Brett and have kept me sober. Living out in the open required submerging myself in those honest conversations that allowed me to find "Brett" in the first place. Those honest conversations taught me that secrets had no place in my life.

Have you ever noticed how often people die for their secrets? We ask government officials to die rather than speak the truth, and we kill people for telling the truth when we wish they would just stay silent. People kill themselves over their own secrets, too. Too often, people would rather end it all than dare to be honest with the people around them. It still scares me that I was nearly one of them.

The forced silence of secrets is inherently isolating. It tells us that there is something — the secret — that is more important than our relationships. It tells us that there are some things we can do better on our own than we can do within a community. The silence of secrets tells us lies. Because all of those are lies. There is nothing we can do better on our own than we can do within a community of people who love us.

Now, I understand that some people, particularly people who are LGBTQ, keep secrets about themselves because it's the only way they can stay safe. I understand and respect that, and of course, I want people to prioritize their personal safety. But those of us who don't have to hide ourselves in the name of safety have to start recognizing how horrible it is that we ask people to choose between their safety and their truths. We have to own the pain that we have been complicit in causing and we have to do everything we can to ensure that we cause no more. I think we can do that by having honest conversations like those in AA; we can do that by sharing our secrets when it's safe for us to do so.

Once I became Brett, perhaps the biggest secret that I realized no longer served me or my community was about my mental health. As I've said before, there were a few people who knew that I dealt with anxiety and depression, but no one knew the extent to which they ruled my life. It wasn't until very recently that I was able to speak candidly about my mental health with even my closest friends.

There was a lot wrapped up in my fear of admitting that anxiety and depression are a part of who I am. The largest issue I have with it is simple: I have an ego problem. I'm aware of it, and likely, most people who are close to me are aware of it too, whether they'd admit it or not. My ego swings like a pendulum from being far too small to being far too large with very short spurts of time in the healthy middle. When my ego is too small, I worry that I'm not good enough for people to love and that if I tell them the truth about my depression they'll realize that. And when my ego is far too big, I'm convinced I can't possibly let people know about my depression because I think they are relying on me to have it *so* much more together than that.

For years, I was afraid to admit how much my heart broke every time I saw another trans person had taken his or her own life. I was afraid that people would know that I'm not so different from those victims of suicide. I was afraid to admit that I know what it's like to be so anxious that I spend an entire day in my bed, or cry for hours for no reason, or even write letters saying goodbye to the people I love. I was afraid of what people would think when they learned (as if they didn't already know) that my transition — my life — hasn't been perfectly smooth. I was afraid that sharing bits about my mental health history would somehow taint my transgender identity. I was afraid that if my post-transition life wasn't an example of something glorious, people would start to doubt whether it was such a good idea after all.

But being Brett—really *being* Brett—was better than a good idea; it was the Creator's perfect idea. And yet, even after journeying into the man that I am today, my depression and anxiety remains. The ways they play out in my actions and thoughts have certainly changed since I've transitioned, and in many ways, they've lessened. I no longer experience many of the social anxieties that used to debilitate me, and my depression is nowhere near as drastic; I can hardly remember the last time my body felt too heavy to go about my day. Neither depression nor anxiety run my life anymore, and yet, there they sit, just beneath the surface, just as much a part of me as my transgender identity.

It's impossible for me to say how much of my mental health is wrapped up in being a transgender man in a world that doesn't want me to exist and how much of it just has to do with the chemicals floating around in my brain. To be honest, I don't really think the "whys" of the situation matter. What matters is that my anxiety and depression are parts of me; they're just as much a part of me as the hair on my head and the scars on my chest. What matters is that our communities are filled with people who are afraid to admit that sometimes they cry and they just don't know why. What matters is that as long as we all pretend it's not a part of us, it will continue to rule us. At the very least, I recognize that I don't know how to break out of its grip unless I admit that it's got a hold on me in the first place.

Nights are the hardest for me. There's just something about the dark—perhaps the fact that we shut ourselves up in our homes away from everyone else, or the fact that in the dark, we physically can't see—that brings out all of the feelings in me. I spend most of my days being rational and guiding each step I take analytically, but there's something about the nighttime that breaks down that method. The night always reminds me that I cannot do this life simply by relying on my brain.

So some nights I call my best friend. I call him, tell him I need to pick him up, and we need to go for a drive. (Thanks to his wife for letting me steal her husband as often as I do.) We drive and we listen to music that makes me realize I'm not alone in the feelings I feel. And he asks all of the right questions to get me to talk about what's happening in my head. Sometimes that shit is like trying to pull your fingers out of a Chinese finger trap: the harder you try, the less progress you make. But most of the time, he knows just what to say to get my head to open up. He reminds me that he loves me. He reminds me that I'm not alone. We hug. We tell each other we're the best friends that could ever be. And then I take him home and I go home finally feeling like I can put my head down on the pillow without fear of what might come in my dreams.

There's just something about being honest with the people who love you.

I used to want to cure my anxiety and depression. It was so buried inside of me and got so little attention or care that I thought the only good thing to do would be to rip it out of me entirely. But I've learned, first, that's impossible to do and, second, that I don't want to. Certainly when they are out of control, my depression and anxiety are not good for me. But my ability to feel and worry about things is not bad in and of itself. It's only bad when I refuse to acknowledge that it's there; it's only bad when I refuse to let others see inside of me, hold me up, and care for me when I don't feel like I can do that myself.

So I just won't anymore. I won't pretend like I'm fine when I'm not. Becoming Brett has taught me that a life unshared—even a life of depression that I sometimes feel ashamed to live—is not a life that is enjoyable, sustainable, healthy, or lovely. I have found so much more beauty in my life since I've been able to admit to and share the parts that I don't find beautiful. Perhaps it's because when I'm honest about the parts of me that hide in the shadows, I think people will know I really mean it when I'm honest about the beautiful, magnificent, and amazingly bright parts.

They say you won't know the light unless you experience the dark, too. I don't believe that for a second. And if the darkness isn't a part of your life, then I thank God for that. But I do believe that, for those of us who live in the dark sometimes, the light gets brighter, and the darkness is less consuming when we share our whole selves.

On The Church

Learning to be honest with yourself and those around you is scary at first, but once you feel the freedom it provides, it can quickly become fun. I've learned to love being honest about who I am. Sometimes it's difficult, but on the whole, it has proven easier than holding on to my secrets. But being honest with yourself almost always means letting go of old dreams and picking up new ones.

I've always been a dreamer. I've always been good at coming up with these huge, elaborate life plans. I'm fulfilling one of them as I write this. But by far, my biggest life plan was to be a pastor in the United Methodist Church. It came to me late one night when I was in the eighth grade. I was lying in bed and thinking about the church. I was thinking about how strange it was that we asked those in need to come to the church for assistance rather than taking assistance to them. It was disconcerting to me how, more often than not, queer people were being chased out of the church rather than welcomed in. My twelve-year-old mind had picked up on a major disconnect between the church and the people we claim to want to serve—one that plagues me to this day. I had an overwhelming knowledge that I was supposed to be a part of the change. I knew in a way that I can only describe as divine revelation that I was supposed to be a leader in the church. I knew that part of what that meant was drawing near to those people that the church liked to keep at a distance. Of course, I didn't know at the time that I was one of those people.

That night, there was something in me that said I was meant to be a pastor. I knew I was supposed to help lead the church through strong theology and excellent pastoral care. I don't know how an eighth grader gets that message. Again, it was divine revelation, I suppose.

Even though I was so young, I had been active in the church for most of my life. I was active in the youth group, I was on youth council, and I had helped my grandpa lead many worship services. I read liturgy, I read theological books that my pastors read in seminary, and I had many theological conversations with pastors and friends. My whole life was saturated in the church and theology, and yet, I was somehow convinced people would think I was an idiot for wanting to be a pastor. I was convinced they'd think I wasn't good enough, smart enough, or the right kind of person to be a pastor.

I have no idea where that kind of self-doubt came from. I had friends, I got good grades, and people seemed to think I was nice. But I was just certain that they were seeing someone who wasn't actually me, and if they really saw me, there was no way in hell they'd think it was a good idea for me to be a pastor.

Because of my fear, there was only one person in the world I felt comfortable talking to about this dream: my grandpa. He had told me many times that he was a troublemaker back when he first thought God wanted him to be a pastor. I remember how people laughed at him when he said that, and I know it hurt him deeply. Because of that, I knew he wouldn't laugh at me; he wouldn't just write me off. But I also expected my grandpa to be honest with me about whether or not this pastor thing was a good idea for me.

I texted him that night. I didn't go into the details about why I thought I was supposed to be a pastor; I just told him I thought I was. He was so supportive of me. He was so careful with my feelings, told me he was proud of me, and to keep listening to how God was directing me.

Eventually, I started telling more and more people that I was going to be a pastor. As time went on, I became more comfortable with that as an identifying aspect of my life. I know there were some people who thought I just liked my pastors and wanted to be like them. I did like my pastors; I thought they were wonderful and lovely people and excellent pastors. But it was more than that for me. I honestly believed then, as I do now, that that desire to be a pastor was from God and not from myself.

That desire—that calling, that whatever-you-want-to-name-it—stuck with me for a long time. It was present during my mess of a high school life, and it was what led me to become a religion major in college—that and a genuine love for theology.

When I was in high school, I started the ordination process in the United Methodist Church for the first time. The process lasts for years, with many meetings with various committees, papers, and a psychological exam. It also requires a Master of Divinity. The sooner I started the process, the sooner I would be able to pastor a church.

But then college happened, and I figured out I was queer, which threw a wrench in all of my plans.

I was in Kansas when I started the ordination process. But as a queer person, Kansas is not where I wanted to attempt to pastor a church. It didn't feel safe—it *wasn't* safe. So while I was in college in Iowa, I found a new church home—a wonderful bilingual congregation in the heart of the capital city. They were so concerned with social justice issues—immigration, food justice, the full-inclusion of LGBTQ people, et cetera—that I fell in love. It's kind of funny looking back: they were *so* progressive theologically that I didn't think I would fit in. But my friend convinced me to keep coming back, and after a few Sundays, they had a hold on me. I've never seen a congregation live out the love of Christ quite like they do. They knew I was trans and still they loved me and affirmed my abilities to preach and lead worship. They told me repeatedly that they thought I would make a great pastor someday. They even convinced me they were right.

The problem is that the United Methodist Church as a whole is not like the congregation I found in Des Moines. Currently, the church's official stance says that being gay or lesbian is incompatible with Christian teaching. It says that being a "practicing" — whatever the hell that means — gay or lesbian person disqualifies you from being an ordained pastor. Of course, there are plenty of queer people who are able to take up official residence behind the pulpit, but there are also plenty of people — too many people — who are shut down with hostility. We put pastors on church trial and strip them of their credentials for officiating queer weddings. And I can't count the number of Annual Conferences in which I have had to listen to disrespectful and harmful conversations about my life and the lives of my queer loved ones and pretend it's "holy conferencing." I saw some holy conferencing, but

I've heard many more conversations that attempt to strip us queer people of our humanity and turn us into an "issue." Our lives, our beating hearts, our blood, and our love are not "issues."

I learned that the pastor life was not the life for me during my orientation at Duke Divinity School. There was a panel on diversity in which four faculty members spoke briefly about the various opportunities at the Divinity School for people in minority groups to get plugged in. They were trying to show that the school is a safe and enjoyable place—even for people who aren't heterosexual, white, upper-class people. As someone who doesn't fit into the stereotypical "Duke" profile, I greatly appreciated the panel. I thought the faculty members did an excellent job making the environment appear safe and welcoming. After each faculty member made opening comments, the floor was opened for questions.

One of the first questions came from a young woman who has since become one of my very best friends. The specifics of her question escape me now, but it had something to do with the LGBTQ community and wanting to ensure that people of that community are safe to express themselves in the Duke Divinity School classroom. A couple of the faculty members addressed the question, and they addressed it well. But moments later, the dean took the stage again. He halted the questions, and he said he wanted to reiterate that Duke is a United Methodist institution. He said that at Duke, we think all people are of sacred worth, but we also uphold the church's stance on homosexuality. He then proceeded to read the church's stance, which states that homosexuality is incompatible with Christian teaching. We were allowed no further questions and directed onto the next part of orientation.

That was the moment that broke me; that was the moment I realized I could not be a pastor in the

United Methodist Church. As he was reading the church's stance, I had flashbacks to the many Annual Conferences where I heard that statement read over and over again. I was outraged. I was outraged that people—including myself—were ostracized at the time when they were supposed to be welcomed. I was outraged that he thought he could speak for the entire ecumenical Divinity School like that. (Despite his words, I have learned that, in fact, the Duke Divinity community does *not* uphold that stance. I have been so welcomed and so loved at Duke, and I have met very few people who think my sexuality or my gender identity is incompatible with Christian teaching.) I was enraged and in so much pain that I realized I couldn't do it anymore. I could no longer willingly and repeatedly put myself in the situation where I had to listen to people tell me my very being is incompatible with the God I love—the God who I know loves me. I could no longer sit in those conversations and pretend they were holy in nature.

I left orientation after that panel and I didn't go back. I was hurt; I felt unsafe and unwelcome. My dear friend, the same one who asked the question that prompted the dean's comments, and I had a great conversation with one of the faculty members on the panel. He was incredibly supportive of us and apologetic about what had happened. I am grateful for him. He was the reason I felt like I could stay and make a place for myself at Duke.

For a while after I realized I couldn't be a pastor, I would tell people I didn't want to be a pastor anymore. I suppose that's partly true. I didn't want to be a United Methodist pastor because I didn't want to intentionally put myself into situations where I knew I wouldn't be cared for.

But the truth is, I did still want to be a pastor...I *do* still want to be a pastor. The sort of divine calling that I felt in eighth grade remains with me to this day. It's still there. I'm still confident that God wants me to be a minister to Her people, and I'm still confident that I would be pretty good at it. But I can't do it because along with my divine call to be a pastor in the United Methodist Church is a divine call to self-care.

Currently, those two callings are incompatible, and that fact breaks my heart. I want to be a church leader. I want to preach good theology. I want to make hospital visits. I want to go to Annual Conferences. I want to go to church council meetings. I want to officiate wedding ceremonies. I want to be able to bless the sacramental elements. Lord, I want to bless the elements. I want to be a pastor of a church that actively welcomes queer people. I want to baptize a lesbian who has come back to the church because we have finally told her that we love her and we are so sorry for what we've done to her. I want to have a naming ceremony for a trans woman who has finally figured out who she is and knows that God (and God's people) love her as herself.

But I cannot do those things. I cannot be myself, love myself, and care for myself and also be a pastor in this church.

Some people have told me that if I'm called to be a pastor, I should just do it despite church discipline. But it's not that simple. It's not simple, easy, or enjoyable to be a pastor in a church that doesn't actively, officially, and publicly support you. I'm grateful for the people who can do it, but I am simply not one of them. Either the health of my parish or my own health would suffer.

There are also plenty of people—liberals and conservatives alike—who have suggested that I leave the United Methodist tradition to be a pastor in one that is more accepting of me. But I am a United Methodist. I'm not a Presbyterian or a member of the United Church of Christ. The

United Methodist Church is my home; it always has been and it likely always will be. That church raised me and made me the man I am—how ironic that the man I am is someone they aren't sure they want.

I will not go anywhere. I will stay in United Methodist pews. I will not be a pastor, but I will be a presence because I have a lot of hope for my church home. There's just something about this church that gives me hope that there is new life on the way.

Despite the pain I have felt from the United Methodist Church, I will defend it when people claim it is unredeemable. But the love and hope that I have for this church is so large that I will not sit silently. I will not stop asking the hard questions: When will we learn that all people are worthy of love and care? When will church trials be a thing of the past? When will we acknowledge that there are trans people in our congregations?

I do not know the answers to any of these questions, and I will not defend our inability to answer them. They are questions that should have easy answers, and I hope that someday they will. But until then, I'm sticking around the church because the conversations won't happen on their own. I'm sticking around because when I came out, I had people in my church offering me resources, love, and hope, and I don't know how not to try to return the favor.

But the dream of being a pastor is one that I have to set down. I have to let it go. It's been a hard task. During all of the years when people usually ask, "What are you going to do with your life?" my answer was always simple: I'm going to be a pastor. My answer is not that simple anymore. In fact, I don't have an answer right now; most of the time, I just feel like I'm ambling through my days with a confused look on my face. I know I have to lay this particular dream down, but I don't yet know what dream I will pick up. Perhaps I will be a firefighter, or a barista, or a househusband, or work in a non-profit.

I don't know what I'm going to do with my life. But I know I'm going to be Brett. And I know I'm going to love myself and do my best to only put myself in places with people who will love and care for me as I love and care for them.

I know I'm going to do my best to love the people around me—especially the queer people who don't get nearly enough love from Christians. I don't know how I'm going to pay my bills. Perhaps it's foolish, but for now, I'm not terribly concerned; I'm just learning how to mourn the dismissal of my dreams, and I'm finally starting to enjoy the task of picking up new ones.

Chapter Four

The Words We Use

I have struggled for a long time with how I could possibly close this book. How does one close a book about a story that is still being lived?

I don't have a tidy, packaged up way to close because I don't have a tidy ending to my story yet—and I probably never will. I'm still breathing, cleaning up my messes, making new messes, having fun, and loving people every day. I don't know how it's all going to turn out or where I'm going to go from here. But this book does have to close, even if my story hasn't yet.

There's something undergirding all that I've written but that I've yet to explicitly acknowledge: *the words we use matter.*

I think the way we talk to and about people has a much greater influence on the way we exist in the world than we like to believe. I know what it's like to hear people talking about you when they think no one else is around. I know that sinking feeling in my gut when someone I thought I could trust has such disregard for the words they use about me. And I know that hearing those words can shut a person down; they can convince a person that truths are safer in one's head than in words falling on the ears of another. I urge you to be cautious with the words you use — even if you think it's a private conversation. The kind of shutting down that harmful words can cause in a person is a dangerous thing for all of us.

I also know what it's like to be on the other end of this situation. I know what it's like to say the words that cut a person. I know what it's like to say the word "fag" around a gay person who was abused by that word when he was growing up. I know what it's like to have to live with the fact that my one word dragged him back to times and places he should have never had to live in even once, let alone repeatedly in his memories. The words we use matter, and we have to start being intentional about them.

For trans people especially, words matter. For a long time, the only way I could show myself love or feel love and support from others was through words—through the words I used about myself and the words others used toward me. The physical transition wasn't immediate for me. I had to rely on people calling me Brett, or using male pronouns, or on people talking to me like they talked to all of their guy friends. That was how I knew it was going to be okay. Without words of affirmation, agreement, and approval, I wouldn't have known that it was okay to be myself.

The words on these pages came out of me freely only because of the words of others. If others had not told me that I could write, that I had a story to tell, that I was worth love, that I *really* was Brett, I would never have found these words—or my life—in the first place. My entire life has opened up before me because the people I love told me it could. Over and over and over again, they told me that I was worth a good life. It took a long time for me to believe them, but their words remained constant nonetheless. My false front of modesty, which was really just self-deprecation, did not slow them down. The words have poured in through whispers, coffee dates, e-mails, texts, phone calls, and handwritten letters. These words have mattered.

The words of others' stories have showed me that there is space in the world for me to tell my own story. These words told me that, even though honest, loving words are scary, there is nothing more valuable.

I have written every single one of these words with great intention. Undoubtedly, some of the words present—or some of the words left absent—will cause harm to one or many of my readers. I'm so very sorry for that. Please know that, while these words were crafted with intention, the harm of another was never a part of my goal in writing. I have tried my best in these pages to tell my own story—and to leave other peoples' stories to their true owners to tell—and I have tried to do so with eloquence and grace. But I know I have not done that perfectly.

This act of taking great care in the words we use is perhaps the most important thing I've learned during my transition. This probably should have been obvious, but it wasn't until I started writing this book that I realized how intentional I want to be in the words I say and write to others. I want the people I care about to know that in my presence they are safe to talk about their addictions and their mental health concerns. I want queer people to know that they can be their true selves around me without fear. I want Christians to know they can have theological conversations with me — even the hard ones that lead to disagreements. I want my future kids to know I will love them no matter what. I want my partner to know she can tell me everything, and that I'll never think she's any less lovely than I did the day I looked into her eyes and told her I loved her for the first time. I want my Mama to know I will always take care of her. And I want all of these people to know all of these things while understanding, and expecting, that the person they will receive when they offer to share their lives with me is truly me — myself, Brett. I don't want them to ever fear that I'm failing to be transparent; I don't want them to have to wonder which version of Brett they're seeing from one day to the next.

I want to offer myself to them — to you. That offering starts in these words. It starts in the words I've written here and the words I will continue to speak. These are honest words; hard words; peaceful words; prayerful words; careful words; calming words; *loving words*.

God, I just want to offer up *loving words* to everyone, but especially to the trans people who are still figuring it out. I'm still figuring it out with you, and I'll do anything I can to make your life easier, safer, and full of love.

God loves you, I love you, and you are so worthy of the very best this world has to offer.

Epilogue

Every year on the national Transgender Day of Remembrance, a list of names circulate. They are the names of transgender people who have died by anti-transgender violence during that year. An unfortunately high number of those individuals are listed as "unidentified." I wrote a letter to the "unidentified persons" for the Reconciling Ministries Network blog, published in 2015. The letter is as follows.

Dear Unidentified Person,

You have a name. You and I both know that. I'm sorry that we have yet to find it. I can't imagine how that breaks your heart.

I remember the first day someone in my family called me by mine. It was a year into my transition and my Grandma sent me an e-mail addressed to

Brett. She said something to this effect: "You probably noticed I wrote this to Brett. It's been a hard year getting to this place, but I want you to know I love you and that I'm with you every step of this journey. Calling you Brett is where I'll start."

I hope you had someone like that; someone who was with you every step of the way.

I hope you felt that feeling of affirmation, love, and compassion when someone called you by your name—not the names you were given, but the name you chose…the name that was yours.

You have a name, even though this piece of paper in my hand doesn't list it. I'm not sure why it's missing, but it's an injustice. It's not fair that such violence was done to you in life, and now in death, people are still turning their backs.

I am sorry. I am sorry that we turned away.

I am sorry that no one stopped whoever caused you harm.

I am sorry that your life didn't end in the amazing love and affirmation that I feel every time my sweet Mom says my name. I am sorry for whatever ways I was complicit in your pain. From the bottom of my heart, I am so sorry.

The least we could do for you is let you have your name, but we didn't. And I know this won't make up for that, but I want to give you a name now. You had the name you chose, but you were also named *Worthy* long before you even knew it to be true—if you ever knew it to be true. You are and were and will always be Worthy. You are Worthy of life. You are Worthy of our love and the love of our Creator. You are Worthy of a safe space to live.

You are beautiful and you are Worthy.

With every breath of my life, I promise you I will try to carry your name on. I will try to show our trans family here and yet to come that, just like you, they are named Worthy.

I will try to be a part of the movement that makes the Body of Christ a safe space for trans people, rather than a space that is nearly as frightening as an alley at midnight.

I will try to stand up to the violence — physical, of course — and the violence of turned backs and awkward stares and not-so-quiet whispers. I will try to show everyone that you, and they, are Worthy.

I will not be perfect. There will be days when I am a part of the violence, and for that, I am sorry. But you have reminded me of what it means to be named Worthy and with that in mind, I will push on through those days when I have been one to cause the hurt.

I long for the day when everyone named Worthy (that is, everyone) can join in communion.

I long for the day when I can give you a hug, call you by your name, and thank you for living as the person God created you to be.

But until then, I will call you Worthy.

With all of my love and with all of my life,

Brett

Connect with Brett Ray

For speaking engagements and book signings, visit **mynameisbrettray.com.** Read more by Brett Ray in publications by Reconciling Ministries Network and Believe Out Loud.

Like the book on Facebook by searching the title and join in the discussion.

Made in the USA
Coppell, TX
07 December 2021